KILLING TIME

The Autobiography of Paul Feyerabend

Paul Feyerabend

These are UNCORRECTED page proofs.
No part of these page proofs may be
reproduced in any form or quoted
without the written permission of
the University of Chicago Press.

ISBN: 0-226-24531-4

Price: $22.95   hardcover
Pages: 224 pp. (est.)   40 halftones

Publication date: May 1995

For additional information, contact:

Rina Ranalli
University of Chicago Press
5801 South Ellis Avenue
Chicago, IL 60637
(312)702-7740

KILLING TIME

THE AUTOBIOGRAPHY OF

PAUL

KILLING
TIME

FEYERABEND

THE UNIVERSITY OF CHICAGO PRESS

Chicago and London

The University of Chicago Press, Chicago 60637
The University of Chicago Press, Ltd., London
©1995 by the University of Chicago
All rights reserved. Published 1995
Printed in the United States of America
04 03 02 01 00 99 98 97 96 95   1 2 3 4 5
ISBN: 0-226-24531-4 (cloth)

CIP data to come

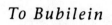
To Bubilein

Einstweilen bis den Bau der Welt
Philosophie zusammenhält,
erhält sie das Getriebe
Durch Hunger und durch Liebe

SCHILLER, *Die Taten der Philosophen,* 1795;
from 1803 better known as *Die Weltweisen*

CONTENTS

1   Family

A few years ago I became interested in my ancestors and the early years of my life. The immediate reason was the fiftieth anniversary of Austria's 1938 unification with Germany. I watched the events from Switzerland, where I happened to be teaching at the time. Austrians had welcomed Hitler with tremendous enthusiasm. Now I heard stern condemnations and resounding humanitarian appeals. Not all of them were dishonest; still, they seemed to be rather futile. I ascribed this to their generality, and I thought that a personal report might be a better way of looking at history. I also was rather curious. After four decades of lecturing at Anglo-American universities I had almost forgotten my years in the Third Reich, first as a student, then as a soldier in France, Yugoslavia, Russia, Poland. Even my parents had become strangers. Who were those people who had brought me up, taught me a language, made me the nervous optimist I still am, and occasionally invade my dreams? And how did it happen that I ended up as an intellectual of sorts, a professor even, with a smooth salary, a crooked reputation, and a wonderful wife?

It is not easy to answer those questions. I never wrote a diary; I do not keep letters, not even from Nobel Prize winners; and I threw away a family album to make room for what I then thought were more important books. The only papers that survived, more by accident than by design, are the birth, marriage, and death certificates of my parents, grandparents, and some great-grandparents.

My father assembled them in 1939, when Austrian civil servants had to prove their Aryan ancestry. Starting from documents already in our possession, he wrote to church registries, used their answers for further inquiries, and worked his way back until the information dried up. I also have the official records of my father's military career, my school reports, administrative details of my service in the German army (*Soldbuch*), and a notebook containing lectures I gave in 1944. Clearing out my office and my wardrobe before my departure for Italy in 1989, I found additional material. There were letters, pocket calendars, bills, telephone numbers, pictures, and documents I had completely forgotten about.

Using this material I can report that my maternal grandfather married a woman twenty years younger than he; that my mother's birth was legitimized twenty-two years after she was born; that my paternal grandfather was the illegitimate son of Helena Feierabend, occupation "houseguest" (*Gästin*); that he replaced the *i* in Feierabend (*Feierabend* is a common word in German, meaning knocking-off time) by the more exotic *y*; and that he married Maria, née Bizjak or Pezjak, a Slovenian national from Bohinjska Bela. I met Maria when I was about seven years old. She sat in the corner of a large room, dressed in the black clothes of a peasant woman. Though already slightly senile she was an imposing presence. Speaking German with a heavy accent she told me the story of her two marriages. "I married a railwayman," she said; "he died; but I *at once*"—and here she raised her voice—"married another railwayman." Then she started all over again. She also told me how she improved her vision by washing her eyes with soapy water. "It hurts—but it makes you see better." This was the only occasion when I saw her. It was long ago and I was a confused little boy; yet I often think of her with sadness and a sense of loss.

My father had two brothers and two sisters. Uncle Kaspar was a baldheaded gentleman with a daring mustache and missing an index finger. He had strong views on almost anything. "Discipline is good for the soul," he said, and hit me. At sixty-five he married a twenty-year-old girl; they divorced when he was sixty-six. Aunt Julie was a dour spinster with a grating voice. She tried to get married but gave it up when one of the prospective husbands departed with her savings. She kept house for us during the war, after my mother had died. When she left, silver spoons, vases, money, sugar, butter, and flour (rare during the war) left with her.

Aunt Agnes was the wife of a station master in Carynthia. We visited them when I was five or six years old. I remember the colorful farm machinery that was being unloaded, the fast train that went by in the afternoon, the restaurant, and the chicken coop behind the station. I spent my days climbing around in the hills above the rails, and I still bear the scars I got from falling down a ravine. Occasionally I went into the chicken coop, closed the gate, and addressed the inmates—excellent preparation for my later profession. One morning Aunt Agnes decided to have chicken for dinner. She locked the kitchen door to keep me away; I grew anxious, smashed the windowpane, and found her with a dead chicken and a lot of blood on her hands. I liberated the remaining birds, fled to the hills, and watched as Aunt Agnes tried to reassemble her flock. In the evenings we all went to the local inn. Papa put me on a table, and I sang the songs my mother had taught me. I got applause, papa got a beer—all on the house.

Papa had participated in the First World War, in Istria, as an officer in the merchant marine. He was discharged because of cholera, which was widespread toward the end of the war. One picture of the family album showed a train with the windows open and occupied by the naked hind-ends of the soldiers; this was the only way to survive a transport. The army documents before me say that papa was proficient in German and Slovenian— yet the only Slovenian word he ever used was *krafl*, "mess." After the war he studied for the lower civil service and moved to the Big

City—Vienna. Mama brought me to his office when I was about nine years old; there he sat, answering questions, certifying copies, signing rental agreements. Not a very important position. But to me he seemed to have enormous power. He loved adventure in his youth; he became rather quiet later on.

After my mother's death, my father ran the household while I was studying at the university. He courted a variety of ladies, some of them married. He visited them at home, or took them out to educational events—lectures, demonstrations, films. Eventually he placed an advertisement: "Civil servant, retired but well preserved, intellectual interests, looking for sensitive mature woman —marriage not excluded." He got eighty replies. I ordered them according to age, income, and style and sent him on his way, twice or three times a week. He returned well fed, inebriated from the rich wines the ladies had saved through the war, and bored to tears. He ended up with a kind but quarrelsome woman and moved to her residence in Bad Ischl. He had a stroke that caused a speech defect and a duodenal ulcer combined with a ruptured peritoneum, which killed him.

We were friends, sort of, but not very close; I was much too self-centered and much too involved in my own affairs. I had already moved to California when I heard of his final illness; I did not return and I did not attend his funeral. Years later, papa appeared in my dreams. I saw him in the distance, wanted to reach him, could not move, and woke up feeling sad and distracted. "Talk to him," said Martina, my beautiful German friend. He came again, standing in a corner, his back toward me. "Papa," I said, "you are a good person; I am grateful for all your care, your patience, your love, the extra efforts you made, and I'm sorry I was such a selfish bastard; I love you." And while I spoke I felt that I indeed loved him and had always loved him. Papa neither moved nor spoke; but he seemed to listen and to accept what I had said. He left and stayed away for a long time.

My mother's family came from Stockerau in southern Austria. There were two sisters, two brothers, and a half brother. Aunt Julie once stayed with us for a few days. I resented her arrival and said so; I was heartbroken when she left. Aunt Pepi was quite beautiful; she drank, became an alcoholic, and committed suicide. Her daughter, my cousin Josephine, found her and came to us. She must have been twelve years old at the time. I can still see the small figure standing in the doorway, asking for help. Mama went and took me along. I remember the neighbors whispering in the corridor, the smell of gas, the motionless shape in the bedroom, and Cousin Josephine saying goodbye from a window when we returned home. I was not upset; I was not puzzled either. I took it for granted that the world was a strange place filled with impenetrable events. I recently returned to the scene, and it seemed as if time had stood still—the same surroundings, the same window, the same impressions, but all the main actors gone. Aunt Pepi often visited us. She also wrote letters, some of them abusive. "She is drunk," mama said. "Does that mean that her writing moves up and down and isn't straight?" I asked. "Yes," mama replied. My memory of things past consists entirely of isolated vignettes such as this one.

Aunt Pepi was married to Konrad Hampapa, a railwayman and a heavy drinker himself. They had two children—Konrad junior, who was retarded, and Josephine. The family visited us on Sundays, and Junior played the accordion. He was an excellent musician and could improvise on any melody he heard. When his father remarried, he tried to make love to his stepmother, Maria. This, he thought, was the normal function of a mother, for Aunt Pepi, apparently, had made love to him. Maria was a kind but determined woman. She stopped her husband's drinking; but she failed with Konrad junior. He left home, roamed the streets, hid in garbage containers (which at the time were large enough to hold ten people), played his instrument, and raped the women who came to listen. He died in an insane asylum at the age of thirty-six—at least this is what I heard later, after my return from London. For me (at age ten), Cousin Konrad was just another relative with a great gift for music. I noticed that he was a little peculiar—but so were many people. My attitude changed when the peculiarity received a name, "retardation," and when casual and unintended hints informed me of its social implications. Fear and revulsion were the result.

Uncle Rudolf was married to a huge Czech woman who loved to gossip about deflowered maidens, aborted children, cuckolded husbands, thieving relatives. She had a sinister face and a sizable mustache, and switched to Czech when the stories got too juicy. One day she forgot. She told my parents how one of our acquaintances had seduced another and how the lady, who seems to have been a virgin, lost "buckets of blood." Buckets of blood! It took a long time for my views of lovemaking to become a little less dramatic. Uncle Rudolf occasionally appeared with a woman closer to his size and complained about the hardships of being married to Aunt Christina. Aunt Christina in turn accused him of trying to poison her. They separated, reunited, separated again; finally Aunt Christina died. Uncle Rudolf, tiny, weak, mousy Uncle Rudolf, lived to be ninety-four.

Uncle Julius was tall and handsome, always ready to play tricks on people. There were vague rumors that he had taken money from a bank, had fled, and had joined the foreign legion. He settled down in Meknes, Morocco, married a Spanish woman, Carmen, and sent us postcards showing him with Carmen, minarets in the background. "Uncle Julius *is* somebody" ("er hat es zu etwas gebracht") was our comment. Uncle Karl, one of my godfathers, was a more shadowy figure. I never met him. He emigrated to the United States, acquired a farm in Iowa, and every year, at my mother's birthday, sent us one dollar. With that mama bought ham, wine, and sweets, and we stuffed ourselves for an entire week.

I also had two cousins, one genuine, the other less so. Cousin Fritz earned his money as a street singer. That was not unusual. In the late twenties the streets and backyards of Vienna looked like amusement parks with organ grinders, animal acts, magicians, dancers, singers—entire bands. They took up their position in the late morning and started tuning their instruments or preparing their equipment. The audience, mostly housewives, made their requests, and the performance began. Salespeople advertised their products with a speech or a song, some outside the house, some on the stairways. Gypsy women sold patchouli wrapped in colored tissue paper. They had a special song, which I still remember. There were accidents; a fire eater burned himself and had to be carried away. Every block had its own beggar who came once a week to collect his dues. "Our" beggar came on Saturdays. When he was through, he went to the butcher downstairs and bought a piece of ham bigger than any one of us could afford.

Cousin Fritz played the guitar and sang, accompanied by a vivacious redhead. I fell in love with her. Inspired by what I had heard about true love, I took an extra pair of shoes ("he packed his bundle," the stories said) and ran away from home. No doubt, I thought, she would be waiting somewhere around the corner, would open her arms and exclaim, "I have been waiting for you all my life." That was another element of the stories I took as my guide. Alas, it did not turn out that way. I got lost (I was five) and was picked up by the police and handed over to my parents. After that, Cousin Fritz and his companion were no longer welcome.

Cousin Emma was a smallish woman, elegant in a cheap way, with a loud voice and many songs in her repertoire. She married a meatpacker, Bautzi Bartunek, a kind but inarticulate gentleman.

On her visits she first sang, even yodeled, then cried a little, then talked about the counts, barons, generals who had laid her. Almost always she concluded by saying, with a gesture toward Bautzi—"and I ended up with this." Bautzi remained quiet, but sometimes he was ready to explode. "One day he will kill her," said papa. It does not seem to have happened. They lived in a tiny dark apartment close to the slaughterhouse; two unhappy people, tied to each other by accidents and disappointed hopes.

When my parents met, mama worked as a seamstress. They married before the First World War, survived the war and the postwar inflation, waited fifteen years until there was enough money for a child—and then produced me. Mama was forty years old when I was born. She had a warm alto voice, and she sang or hummed folk songs every hour, every day. She fell silent when we moved to a "better" neighborhood. Once she told me how, while working as a salesgirl, she had drawn a picture, and a customer, "a dashing gentleman," had complimented her on her talent. That was long ago, the story implied, and now the talent was wasted and life was just routine.

She tried to commit suicide twice. On the first occasion my father and I were out for a walk. It was evening; the gaslights were being turned on, but one of the pilots failed and the flame emitted a mournful sound. I got frightened and urged papa to run home. Mama was in a corner, unconscious, amid a cloud of gas. She succeeded thirteen years later. Often she would run toward the window in a mad rage; I had to use all my strength to prevent her from jumping. Many years after her death, when preparing the furniture for sale, I found her handwriting on the backside of the large bedroom mirror and the wardrobes. "God help me," it said, "I cannot go on."

Meeting my mother in a dream is never a simple matter. She may be kind, she may smile, but I have to be careful, I have to

watch every word and every gesture for madness, and hints of sex-
uality are never far away. More than once I dreamed that I married
an older woman, a very old woman, in fact, and asked myself how
I could get out of the disaster. Still, I made love to her, without
much pleasure, even with revulsion—it was my mother in one of
her many disguises. On other occasions I felt that I was not alone,
that I could pick up the telephone and call her. I tried talking to
mama as I had talked to papa; I did not succeed—until recently, in
Switzerland. I dreamed I was sitting at a bar with Grazia, who is
now my wife; it was dark and I felt uncomfortable. There was
something sinister about Grazia—as if she were about to change. I
became afraid and woke up. "That was mama doing her tricks
again," I said to myself. Trying to go back to sleep, I mumbled,
"Why don't you speak to me?" She appeared while I was still
awake. It was mother all right—but with all her humanity gone. A
scream of rage and despair had torn her face and corroded her features. Visually, the image was quite weak, barely noticeable, about
five inches in diameter; but the impact was terrifying. The image
lingered at the foot of my bed for about a minute and then disappeared.

A few months later, on Monday, September 11, 1989, to be ex-
act, I discovered mama's suicide note. I was in my office at school
talking to Denise Russell, a friend from Australia. I was going
through my filing cabinets. I had not looked at them for at least
fifteen years—but I wanted to clear them out before leaving for
Italy. I opened the top drawer. There were some offprints, old tax
forms, and about ten pocket calendars. One of these contained
some photographs and the note. I could hardly believe my eyes. I
didn't know that such a note existed—and then I remembered,
yes, I had seen it long ago but had forgotten about it. I explained
its content to Denise, went to my seminar, two hours, hurried
home, and took a close look. The note is addressed to my father.

There is no anger, no madness; only love and a desire for peace. Holding the letter in my hand, I for the first time felt close to that strange, distant, and unhappy human being that had been my mother.

2   Growing Up

The first apartment I remember had three rooms: a kitchen, a bed-sitting-room, and a study. The kitchen and the bed-sitting room are fairly clear in my mind; the study is a mystery. I went in occasionally, but I never really saw it. Here my father received visitors and kept his belongings. Below was a carpenter's workshop, above a seamstress. I often got scared when I heard the sound of her sewing machine. Even today an unknown noise disturbs me until I know exactly how it is produced.

We lived in the Wolfganggasse, a quiet street lined with oak trees. Downstairs were a butcher and a grocery; the drugstore was at the corner opposite. The whole block rejoiced when the owner's son, a fat, serious boy, finished high school; he now belonged to a higher plane, different from the rest of us. After the drugstore came the police station. Mama and I went there once when papa did not show up for dinner. Papa was all right; he had been out with his colleagues.

Farther down was an avenue with streetcars, traffic, and larger stores. That was the end of the world as far as I was concerned.

Years later, in the 1960s, when I was already teaching in California, I started dreaming about the apartment; it was eerily empty, and an important part of my life seemed to have been lost there forever. To resolve the puzzle I visited the place around 1965. I took a tram to the Gürtel, walked across Haydn Park, where I had played as a child, passed the corner with the movie theater—now

11

replaced by a department store—and approached our old quarters. I felt nervous and tense. There were the oak trees, there was our house, there was the door. It was closed. I opened it and went in. The hall was dark and cool. I looked around. No response. I walked up one floor and went toward one of the apartments—no, ours was on the third floor. I moved up to the third floor, around the corner, and finally stood in front of number 12. Our apartment. Everything looked as it had looked in the dream—void, and yet by its very emptiness a remembrance of a life that had ceased long ago. The problem was right in front of me, but I could not solve it. (It dissolved in 1990 when I returned with Grazia. The apartment no longer existed: the house had been completely rebuilt.)

Between the ages of three and six I spent most of my time in the kitchen and in the bedroom. Mama moved a bench up to the window and tied me to the windowframe. There I hung like a spider and watched the world: major street repairs, colorful steamrollers, the green electric buses that transported the mail, the street performers, and now and then a private car. Once a week a bunch of pigs was delivered to the butcher's shop in the house opposite. On Friday the workers received their paychecks, went to the local pub, and got drunk. Between two and three in the morning—I was in bed at the time, but the noise woke us all up—their wives went looking for them and brought them home. It was an impressive sight: huge women lifting tiny men up by their collars and shouting with thunderous voices: "You heap of shit! You bum! You asshole! Where's the money? . . ." Even the mailman ended up in the gutter with letters, checks, bills scattered all around him.

Inside, wives beat their husbands (and vice versa), parents beat their children (and vice versa), neighbors beat each other. Every morning the ladies of the house assembled at the bassena, the only water outlet on each floor. They exchanged gossip, commiserated, complained about their men, pets, relatives. Most of the time that was that. Once in a while the gossip increased in volume, changed character, and turned into a row. Endearments such as "You whore! You bitch!" filled the corridors. Weapons (brooms and so forth) might be added, but dragging the opponent around by her hair seemed to suffice. Turds on the stairway meant that the janitor had managed to make an enemy or two. It would be wrong to infer that our house was an extreme case, however. The nuns at a well-known Catholic hospital where I had my appendix removed used the same language and treated each other in almost the same way.

Festivities (Easter, or Christmas) were severe tests of moral fiber. For days before, the ladies would wander from butcher to grocer to baker to wine merchant, shopping for food; their husbands came home with secretive smiles on their faces and parcels hidden behind their backs. There was much moving around in the kitchens and in the back rooms. At last the great day arrived. Cooking started early in the morning; bewitching smells spread all over the house. The families assembled, tasted the food, and had dinner accompanied by animated conversation. Presents further improved the climate; happiness and goodwill flowed in abundance. The stage was set. Somebody made an unfortunate remark; an astonished silence followed. Somebody else replied, increasing the temperature a little. Soothing voices intervened—to no avail. Insults proliferated until there was an all-out fight. Next day everybody slept until noon. I cannot say that our family was above such behavior—still, most holidays were pure magic.

Take Christmas! Weeks in advance I began filling a booklet my father had put together from loose sheets with pictures, numbers, notes: "23 days to Christmas"—accompanied by a drawing; "22 days to Christmas"—followed by some illegible scribbling; and so on. I loved to cover clean white paper with colors, lines, words. In time, I wrote a detailed letter and left it in the flowerbox outside the window. And then the great day arrived—Christmas Eve. Papa looked out of the window. "I don't know," he said; "your letter is still here; I hope the Christmas angel has not forgotten our apartment." "Can't you tell him?" I asked. "One doesn't tell an angel how to run his business; if he comes, he comes; if he doesn't come—well, what can we do?" Later in the day papa locked himself into the sitting room, "just to be on the safe side." Evening came; the door opened; there were the lights, the tree, the smell of sweets, the presents—it was pure magic.

Once a month mama took me to Schönbrunn, the former summer residence of the Austro-Hungarian emperors. She put me in a pram and wheeled me to the entrance, and I pushed the vehicle the rest of the way. I remember standing between the handles of the pram, trying hard to make it move. I also remember being photographed with the Gloriette, an open-air building, in the background. Photographers back then had a variety of tricks to keep children still. Mine used a stuffed bird; it appeared from nowhere and I stared at it in amazement. I have seen the photo: a fat little monster wrapped in layers and layers of warming material and looking utterly stupid. "You can tell his face from his bottom because it's where the noise comes from," people said.

On the way back we passed apartment houses occupied by soldiers. The soldiers often threw loaves of bread to the people below—food was scarce in the twenties. On Sundays papa, mama, and I went camping at a meadow at the edge of town. We took food, a blanket, and swimming suits and stayed the whole day. I liked moving around, and I especially liked sitting at the feet of girls who were twelve to sixteen years old (I was three to six at the time). Seeing the admiration in my eyes, they welcomed me, very much to the disgust of their boyfriends, who became sullen and nasty. Papa used the situation to his advantage. "This is my boy," he said; "What a cute boy!" said the girls—and so the conversation proceeded. I even got a kiss now and then. In the evening, suffering from a sunburn, I lay in my bed, embraced myself, and thought of the beautiful faces that had been so close to mine.

I often accompanied my mother to the hairdresser. "What do you want to do when you grow up?" asked the ladies. "I want to retire," I replied. There was reason in my reply. Building sandcastles in the park I saw nervous men with briefcases running after crowded streetcars. "What are those people doing?" I asked mama. "They're going to work," she said. I also saw an elderly gentleman sitting quietly on a bench, enjoying the sun. "Why is he here?" I asked. "He is retired." Well, after that, retirement looked very attractive indeed.

Occasionally mama took me to the movie house on the corner. Some of the films were funny; others were perplexing and a bit sinister. For example: a soldier returns from the war (the First World War). His wife embraces him; he pushes her away; "Kiss him!" he says, pointing at his son. I felt the tension between the man and the woman, the implied cruelty, but I also felt that the woman wanted it that way and that she was doomed because of her desire. That, at least, is how I would describe my feelings today. At the time, all the elements were tied together in a big, puzzling knot. I remember our immediate neighbors, the old woman, and younger woman (Frau Mazernitz), her husband (practically invisible), the daughter, Steffi, who slowly grew up, filled out, and started dating. I did not know the other neighbors very well and I knew the streets even less. The world is a dangerous place, said my parents, and kept me home. They did not even allow me to go to the toilet; we had one public toilet on each floor, none in the apartments; and I was put on a chamberpot until I was nine years old.

During my first five years I took a nap at one o'clock every afternoon. I once dismantled the alarm clock that was supposed to wake me up and put it together again before falling asleep. I also played a little accordion, and I played it rather well. Nobody paid attention. Thus a talent I may have possessed gradually eroded. I was often sick with stomachache or a fever. I had a nervous affliction, similar to epileptic fits: my eyes rolled up, I made strange noises and fell to the ground (at fifteen I added sleepwalking to my repertoire). The doctor was hardly ever called—mothers were supposed to know the elements of health care. Fever, for example, was treated by wrapping the patient in hot towels, pouring hot lemonade (with or without an aspirin) down his throat, and letting nature do the rest. More than once I almost died sweating out a cold. Pains were no big deal; "They will soon go away," my parents said. This approach was certainly more rational than appealing to specialists for every trifle—but there were disadvantages. For years I had stomach pains, occasionally so acute that I rolled around on the floor; finally, a doctor diagnosed an inflamed appendix, enlarged and close to perforating. Once—I must have been ten—my mother took me to a psychiatrist; at least I think he was a psychiatrist, and the reason, I think, was bedwetting. A small man with a bald head and shiny eyeglasses, he oozed benevolence. He examined me and then took my mother to an adjoining room. When he reappeared, he looked mean and threatening. He really scared me, but I don't know if that stopped whatever it was that had made mama bring me to him.

I started school when I was six. It was a strange experience. Having been kept off the streets, I had no idea how other people lived or what to do with them. Papa gave me his military knapsack instead of the customary briefcase. "People will envy you," he explained. I was laughed at. "Defend yourself!" said mama. Next day I did just that. School was over and I started for home. I saw mama at the window, remembered her advice, turned to the main offender, and broke his arm. Gradually things settled down and instruction began. Now I could not understand why I should sit still while the teacher was wandering around; so I wandered around with him. He ordered me back to my place. There I remained, but I began to throw up as soon as the first letters appeared on the blackboard. I was sent home and cleaned; papa issued a solemn warning: "Don't repeat this performance, or you'll get it!" Again I was in school, sitting in my place, trying to stay calm; again the teacher went to the blackboard, wrote a few letters, and again I threw up. "He's not ready for school," said the teacher. "Bring him back next year." "He'll settle down," said papa; "it's just one of those things." And so it was. After two weeks I became accustomed to the new life and enjoyed it. Two years later I even had to change classes; my teacher, Fräulein Wunderer, complained that I was too tough for her. I have no idea what prompted the complaint, but it seems that my problems had disappeared. I shudder when I think what an American Child Psychiatrist might have done to me.

I have often tried to figure out how I learned to read. There must have been a time when I could not read, then an intermediate stage when I could read a little, and finally, a stage when I could read very well. At least that's what I thought later on. But I simply cannot identify the stages. It seems that I could read when I entered school, but I don't know how I learned. Papa had bought a variety of comic books. The characters talked; what they said was contained in a bubble above their heads. I may have learned reading from figuring out what was in the bubble. Without any great effort. I also remember how vivid the drawings were; they lived, acted, almost leaped off the page. Here was another world, real, and full of mystery. I also had an encyclopedia with pictures of animals, plants, cities. Some plants looked OK. Others were threatening, and I quickly turned the page.

Once a year papa took us to the Prater, the local funfair with carousels, rollercoasters, and a complete miniature town run by midgets. The magic train was my favorite. Standing outside between journeys it looked quite innocuous—little carriages with plain seats and simple patterns. Papa bought a ticket; we sat down and waited. At last the train started moving; it drove into a grotto and then, after some ominous darkness, a marvelous view opened up on the right, a monstrous creature attacked from the left, spiderwebs fell onto your face, hands reached out and tried to touch us.

Years later I took the same train, but all I saw were the shabby seats, the badly constructed cities, the ridiculous paper monster.

And comics are just drawings. They may be funny and interesting—I still get a kick out of them—but they no longer live. Even stories have changed their character. I remember a story about a man and a fly. The man sits in his room, reading. The fly disturbs him with its buzzing. The man looks around, sees the fly, moves up to it; the fly disappears and silence returns. The man sits down and resumes reading. Again the fly disturbs him . . . and so on. I thought that the fly was a special fly, that it had dissolved into nothing and had recombined. I can imagine a fly like that today and I can imagine some adventures it might get involved in. But it would be fiction; the air of reality would be gone. Is it surprising that I dislike reformers like Brecht who turn the theater, one of the last strongholds of magic, into a sociological laboratory?

Once a year, on December 10, my father dressed up (at a neighbor's) in a bishop's outfit, put on a mask, and entered our place as Saint Nicholas. Mama and I waited in the kitchen. There was a knock. "It must be Saint Nicholas," said mama. I trembled with fear and excitement. Mama opened the door and Saint Nicholas came in. I knelt down. Papa asked in a deep voice: "Have you been a good boy? Have you done your homework? Did you obey your parents?" And I had to admit, alas, that I had sinned here and been negligent there and that my behavior had been far from exemplary. Saint Nick came closer, looked at me with a penetrating glance, hit me (gently, of course), and said: "Next time you won't get away that easily"; and then he departed. Outside the door he left a basket with fruit, chocolate, and various sweets.

When my father returned, he looked exhausted; he had a leather strap in his hand and explained how he had caught, tied, and gagged the devil while Saint Nick was giving me the third degree. "You know," he said, "you were lucky; this time the devil almost got away and he surely would have beaten you up. He might even have taken you with him!" I believed the story, especially as the neighbors were moving around in the corridor in demonic costumes. "Poor papa," I said. I gave him some of my presents and was proud of the strength that had enabled him to restrain the Evil One himself. Mama told stories about angels and devils, and I often interrupted with inventions of my own. One story was about a clever man who sold his soul, regretted the bargain, and lured the hot devil onto a frozen lake; the ice melted, the devil sank, and the man was free. This, I think, was my idea.

I firmly believed in angels and demons. They could turn up anywhere and do anything. I was afraid of God. He was far away and rather colorless—he merely *was*—but he was also powerful and knew the most hidden events. Before Holy Communion I went to confession not only once, but two or three times—too many bad thoughts had invaded me in the meantime. (To avoid being bothered the priest soon absolved me from all sins I might commit between confession and communion.) Words and events that could have changed my attitude made no impression whatsoever; I noticed them, but I did not connect them with my beliefs. Once, at school—I was seven years old—I witnessed a strange scene. One of the boys went up to the teacher and shouted, with tears in his eyes, "There are no angels! They don't bring the Christmas presents! It's a trick, done by the parents!" I remember the scene very clearly; I can identify the boy from a photograph that seems to have survived my travels and periodic attempts at housecleaning. Yet it meant absolutely nothing to me. I was not shocked; I didn't change my mind. I simply had no idea what the fuss was about. As far as I was concerned it was one of the

many strange events that seemed to make up our world. (The dead
bodies and the blood-spattered streets I saw in Vienna during the
civil war of 1934 and the events of the Nazi period affected me or,
rather, failed to affect me in exactly the same way.)

In 1932 Saint Nicholas appeared for the last time. I was eight
years old and we had already moved to our new apartment. Again
it was the tenth of December. Again I waited. I was alone, reading
Viennese legends. One of the legends explains why Saint Stephen's Church has one finished tower and a mere stump for the
other: the master mason was overwhelmed by the magnitude of
the task and asked the devil for assistance. "Yes," said the devil, "if
you give me your soul." The mason agreed; then he tried to get out
of the bargain. The devil flung him from the scaffolding; after that
nobody dared to finish the church. Suddenly I heard steps in the
anteroom—my father? Saint Nicholas? I had an inkling that
things were not what they used to be and yet I was not sure about
the difference. The door opened. Here was the old familiar figure:
the long white dress, the golden embroidery, the staff, the pointed
hat, the deep voice. But I also saw my father's shoes, which I had
not noticed before, I saw the eyes behind the mask, which I had
never separated from the mask, and I heard him, not Saint
Nicholas. It was my father; clearly it was my father, yet equally
clearly it was not my father but the Saint.

Homer describes many situations of this kind. Aphrodite appears as an old woman; but Helen, whom she addresses, also sees
"the round sweet throat of the goddess"; the second appearance
does not eliminate the first, it adds to it. This was exactly what
happened to me, for a short time at least; then the mystery disappeared and I was left with the commonplace. I was sad, not for myself but for my father, who, having been a mighty Saint, was now a
vulnerable human being.

3   High School

There were three types of high school: the classical *Gymnasium* with Greek, Latin, and literature; the *Realschule* with modern languages and science; and a mixture, the *Realgymnasium,* with eight years of Latin, no Greek, and a choice between science and French in the fifth year (English was being taught in either case). After some discussion papa chose the *Realgymnasium.* I tried to adopt a suitable attitude. A high school student, I said to myself, is somebody who knows. People who know, I continued, can be recognized from their looks and their behavior. For a few days I walked around with measured steps and a mean look on my face; then my lazy disposition got the upper hand. The entrance exam was rather mild. I read the story of a woman who almost starved searching a wood for her lost child. Halfway into the story the examiner asked: "And what is such behavior called?" "Mother-love," I replied, which was the correct answer. I got a toy boat as a reward and blocked the bathtub for at least a week. I was ten years old and obviously very different from the geniuses who read Bourbaki in their prams.

High school in Germany in the thirties differed from high school in the United States and from some recent Continental schools. Instruction started at 8:00 A.M. and lasted four or five hours. Each hour another gentleman entered the classroom and tried to turn us into articulate and civilized human beings. The first forty-five minutes might be Latin; then a fifteen-minute break; after that forty-five minutes of mathematics; again a fifteen-minute break—and so on until noon or one o'clock. Some teachers kept us quiet by their mere presence; others amazed us by their bizarre behavior; still others threatened us, got red in the face, stamped their feet; they were the least successful.

Instruction included repetitions and examinations. I did rather well in these games, though I frequently dreamed of having forgotten the schedule for a particular day and entering the classroom ignorant and fearful. Later, when about sixteen, I had the reputation of knowing more physics and mathematics than our physics and mathematics teachers; they seemed to believe the rumors and left me alone. Biologists and chemists did the same; they were in awe of physics and therefore of me. Needless to say, I neglected the assigned books and daydreamed in class. During question time I assumed a knowing and slightly bored attitude as if trivialities such as these were beneath me. It worked—but I had uncomfortable moments. Teachers do not always act in a rational manner, so what if Mr. Cerny, under stress, should suddenly decide to ask me about aromatic and aliphatic compounds? Even at the university I sailed through chemistry courses without answering a single question. "You physicists know everything," said the examiner, a well-known organic chemist, and gave me the top grade. Slowly my reputation went to my head. "Do you think you know more physics than Professor Thomas?" a friend inquired when I was twelve. I considered the matter for a long time and finally admitted that Professor Thomas might know just a tiny bit more than I. In 1939, when the first newspaper reports appeared about the Hahn-Strassmann discovery, I was asked: "Do you think this is possible?" I again immersed myself in deep thought and finally declared that, no, it was not possible.

I was a *Vorzugsschüler,* that is, a student whose grades exceeded a certain average. In the yearly reports this was indicated by a star next to my name. Such achievements did not contribute to popularity. "Specialists"—students who excelled in, say, history, or mathematics, or chemistry—were respected; their knowledge, we assumed, was the result of interest combined with intelligence. Besides, they had an important function during question time when they provided a rich flow of illegitimate information; and they kept the teachers in place by exposing their errors. But excellence in all fields looked like an urge to conform. Fortunately I was often reprimanded and once even thrown out of school. One could trust a guy like that.

I had a few friends, and I was in love with some of them. I would accompany them home or linger in their neighborhood until they appeared, and then I would turn up as if by accident. I longed for physical contact but was much too shy to make a move. I shrank back when one of my classmates, a good-looking and fiery-eyed boy, reached between my legs. I admired girls from a distance and imagined rescuing them from sticky situations. There was a lady who lived close to our house whom I saw every morning on my way to school. She was pale, mysterious, and beautiful, about sixteen years old; surely she was the helpless and unwilling slave of an evil man with a cruelly thin mustache! One day, I thought, she would approach me, tell me of her troubles, and I, with an elegant gesture, would reduce her tormentor's power and set her free.

I thrived on sentimental movies (I still do). The elements were always the same: an unhappy woman, a good guy who didn't dare open his mouth, and a bastard who profited from the silence. "Why don't they talk to each other?" I asked myself; "it's so simple. Why do they suffer when a single word could solve their problems?" And I imagined entering the screen, saying the word, and leaving, being loved for the rest of my life by the woman I had liberated. Magda Schneider, the mother of Romy Schneider and Sylvia Sydney, frequently benefited from my interventions.

In summertime the family moved to a farm. We got bed and

board and helped with the work. I took the cows out to graze, my
father and I collected the hay, and I hung around the resident
ladies. The first time we were there, I was twelve and the lady was
eighteen, a strong and cheerful country girl. I accompanied her to
town and back and talked her ears off. I have a picture of both of us
sitting on a boulder, she with her arm around me, I with a big,
happy smile. The next time I was thirteen and the lady must have
been about thirty. Her name was Vilma; she was from Yugoslavia
and spoke hardly any German. She cleaned the stables and prepared the feed for the pigs. Noticing my admiration, she invited
me to call her by her first name. An entire ceremony is connected
with such a change: the parties fill their glasses with wine, entwine
their arms, with glass in hand, empty their glasses, and then kiss.
We had only cider, but we kissed and I felt in seventh heaven.
Once I saw Vilma in the corridor in front of the stables, looking
straight ahead and cleaning a pair of shoes. I thought I had never
seen anyone so beautiful. Most likely she was an ordinary woman,
perhaps even ugly—but what do love and admiration care about
such abstract judgments as these? I went with her to the fields, sat
by her side, and looked at her. The other workers—all women,
many of them Gypsies—laughed and made some rather obvious
sexual remarks. I had no idea what they were talking about. Next
time I was fourteen and the object of my admiration was twelve. I
borrowed an oxcart with two oxen (I was an excellent oxcart
driver) and drove around with her. Or we simply sat in the driver's
seat, embraced, and kissed. Mama had a fit: "You scoundrel, you
filthy swine!" she screamed. Papa, greatly embarrassed, asked,
"Did you approach the girl in any way?" Again I had no idea what
he meant, but I can still see his kind and troubled face.

   I loved the dark nights in the countryside; nothing to see, but
mysterious noises everywhere. I loved thunderstorms; hearing
them on their way, I ran out into the fields and yelled at the sky.
The farmers got angry and dragged me back into the house: "You

stupid boy! Don't you know that God punishes those who challenge him?" Lacking a well-defined character (not being "internally referenced," as psychologists say), I readily adopted rural habits and patterns of speech. They faded after a few days back in the city. The visits stopped when I was about fifteen. From then on we stayed in Vienna, and I was left to my own resources.

We had moved to a "better neighborhood," so my parents allowed me to play with the children in the street. I rolled around on a contraption consisting of a board, two wheels, and an upright extension for steering, took part in a game called "jumping the temple," and once gave all my savings to a girl who had asked me for money. Mama was furious; she went to the girl's parents, made a fuss, and retrieved the money—which hardly made me popular with the locals. I also read a lot. I have no idea how and why it started, but I do know that when about nine I had an open book in front of me almost every evening. First children's books. The events in *Der Struwwelpeter*—the tailor who cuts off the thumbs of thumbsucking children, the huntsman who gets shot by a hare, the boy who dies because he won't eat his soup—seemed rather commonplace; however, I was puzzled by the introduction, in which the author, a pediatrician, explained why he had written the book and how it should be used. That was mysterious stuff indeed! I shall never forget the sad story of Rübezahl, the deceived giant. He was in love with a beautiful princess. "What can I do for you?" Rübezahl asked the princess. "Count the turnips in my garden," the princess replied, knowing very well that counting was not one of the giant's strengths. He counted and counted, made mistakes, started again. People from all over the country mocked him and called him Rübezahl, "turnip counter." Eventually he got the joke, uttered a frightful curse, withdrew to the woods, and swore never to come out again. Now Rübezahl had a good heart and hated injustice; people looked for him when they needed help. They still called him Rübezahl since this was the only name they knew. When he appeared, he was fuming, ready to kill. It took speed and eloquence to turn his anger at the insult into anger at the injustice he was supposed to remove. What an intriguing story, I thought; the only way to get help is to risk your life, offend the powers that can help you, and quickly turn their thoughts to other matters.

I read *Don Quixote* (in a children's edition), legends, fairy tales. When I ran out of books, I went to the local library. I borrowed Zane Grey, Edgar Wallace, Conan Doyle, Alexandre Dumas, Marie Ebner Eschenbach, Jules Verne, Hedwig Courts-Mahler, even Pitigrilli, though his stories were beyond me. I may have read Schnitzler (his novels or monologues, not his plays), but I am not sure. I burst into tears over *Uncle Tom's Cabin* and often could not sleep after a dramatic tale. "You mustn't read that stuff," papa would say, and he would hide the books for a day or two. I read almost all of Karl May, a German writer of adventure stories who described countries he had never seen and people he had never met. His Indians are noble creatures, superior to their white visitors both in strength and in wisdom, his Arabs courageous but wily customers. A few years ago I read May again and discovered the secret of his success: brief expositions, colorful descriptions, no lingering on inessentials (such as character development or social background). For May, character is what character does, and character always does good, or bad, but at any rate interesting things and, moreover, does them quickly and decisively. I tried to write adventure stories of my own; I succeeded in getting my heroes into impossible situations; I rarely succeeded in getting them out.

Somehow I stumbled into drama and philosophy. We read drama in high school, different parts being assigned to different students. I enlarged my characters to gigantic dimensions; good people oozed benevolence, bad people were evil personified. Needing further material for expressing this talent I bought paperbacks of Goethe, Schiller, Grabbe, Kleist, Shakespeare (the Schlegel-

Tieck translation), and Ibsen and took them on long walks in the woods and hills around Vienna. I had special places in secluded areas; there I sat, or strutted around, read and declaimed for hours. Peer Gynt and Faust were my heroes; the Dovregybben, Mephisto, Shylock, Richard III my favorite dramatic parts. I soon knew *Faust, Part One* by heart; I often recited the sunset passage at the beginning of the drama and Mephisto's deception at the end of *Part II*. I liked the easy rhymes (in Passarge's translation) of Ibsen's early plays, but I had no use for *Iphigenie* or the *Bride of Messina*. I was offended when action—good, absorbing, juicy action—was diluted by an action-free interest in form, and I skipped the passages where the characters bared their souls. I still prefer writers who let events take their course to those for whom poetry or self-revelation or social analysis takes the front seat. For a long time this preference put mysteries at the top of my list. Unfortunately even these innocent stories are now being invaded by "meaning."

Philosophy entered by sheer accident. I bought most of my paperbacks secondhand. I also went to pre-auction sales, where tons of books could be had for a few pennies. They came in bundles; you had to buy a whole bundle or nothing at all. I selected bundles that were rich in plays or novels, but I could not avoid an occasional Plato, Descartes, or Büchner (the materialist, not the poet). I may have started reading these unwanted additions out of curiosity or simply to cut my losses. I soon realized the dramatic possibilities of reasoning and was fascinated by the power that arguments seem to exert over people. Having digested a few pages of Descartes's *Meditations*, I explained to mama that she existed only because I existed and that without me she did not have a chance. (During the war I presented the same argument at the officers' school in Dessau-Rosslau; the well-uniformed gentlemen in my audience did not know what to make of it.) Altogether, my interests were rather unfocused (they still are). A book, a film, a theatrical performance, or a casual remark could move me in any direction. I remember visiting one of our German teachers, Professor Wiener, at his home. He corrected the soggy religious poetry I produced when I was twelve and tried to give structure to my literary ambitions. He had many books, three blue volumes on chemistry among them. The color alone sufficed to attract me to that subject.

My interest in physics and astronomy came from an excellent physics teacher at our school, Professor Oswald Thomas, a well-known figure in Viennese adult education. Once a month, Thomas assembled about two thousand people in a large meadow outside Vienna, turned off the streetlights, and explained the constellations. He told scientific details about the stars and somewhat less scientific stories about the legendary animals, gods, humans that populated the sky. He was elegant, with graying hair, shiny eyeglasses, a charming accent (he came from Siebenbürgen in Hungary), and a wicked sense of humor; ladies of all ages were in love with him. He also gave lectures at his office and at the university. I attended most of them and assisted him in various ways. On my thirteenth birthday I was permitted to give a lecture of my own. "Two minutes," said Professor Thomas; I had to be removed after ten.

Oswald Thomas wrote one of the best popular astronomy books I know: *Astronomie: Tatsachen und Probleme* (Astronomy: Facts and Problems). His style, though concise and factual, was radiant and captivating. Even the most pedestrian facts became as enchanting as fairy tales. Airy, Tyndall, Jeans, and Eddington were his models. Starting with the geocentric view of the universe, Thomas explained the various reference systems and enumerated the phenomena that occurred in them. With the help of excellent diagrams he described planetary and stellar motions, including the major lunar perturbations. A whole system of detailed and precise astronomical knowledge arose without a single word about the motion of the Earth. Causal accounts were introduced later and were then relativized by cosmology. I also saw that highly abstract concepts could be explained in an informal way, and I tried my luck with the special theory of relativity. I did not succeed. (Hermann Bondi with his *k*-calculus has now almost solved the problem.)

Inspired by Thomas's book and a pair of mirrors advertised in a popular scientific journal, papa and I built a telescope from a bicycle and an old clothing stand. I now became a regular observer for the Swiss Institute of Solar Research. I projected the sun onto a screen, made a sketch of the distribution of the sunspots, counted individual spots and groups, calculated the "solar spot number" (the sum of all the individual spots plus ten times the number of the groups), and mailed the result. I also read advanced treatises so as to understand more technical arguments. And I coached students in Latin and mathematics to get money for books. Volume 3 of Adolf Wüllner's old *Lehrbuch der Experimentalphysik* (1899–1902) was my first textbook. It is an enormous tome, 1400 pages long, with many illustrations. I worked my way through it, page by page, from beginning to end. I had trouble with potential theory, which was explained in the first chapter (up to and including Poisson's equation). I understood the formulas and could follow the derivations, but I did not understand what the theory was about. What was this strange magnitude, the potential, which played such an important role in mechanics and electrodynamics and turned up in so many special cases? The difficulty disappeared when I learned vector calculus. The calculations were shorter, the ideas more intuitive—and that seemed to settle the matter: the potential was nothing but an auxiliary magnitude introduced to simplify the calculation of forces. (The problem was far from solved, however. The Bohm-Aharonov effect and gauge invariance show that the alleged Hilfsgrösse contains features that can be activated by novel assumptions.) I read many volumes of the famous Göschen series, Bechert-Gehrtsen's *Atomic Physics* and

Knopp's *Theory of Functions* among them. It was hard work. Lacking the ability to divine the ideas behind a complicated calculation, I have to go over explanations repeatedly, step by step, until some kind of sense emerges. Since I was aware of this shortcoming, I realized very early that I had no natural talent for mathematics. Undeterred, I simply worked harder—and was rewarded. I still remember the elation I felt when, after much reading back and forth, the import of the Cauchy-Riemann differential equations for complex functions suddenly dawned on me.

I was interested in both the technical and the more general aspects of physics and astronomy, but I drew no distinction between them. For me, Eddington, Mach (his *Mechanics* and *Theory of Heat*), and Hugo Dingler (*Foundations of Geometry*) were scientists who moved freely from one end of their subject to the other. I read Mach very carefully and made many notes. Then I forgot about him. Decades later I heard Mach described as a short-sighted and narrow-minded positivist. "That is not the Mach I know," I said, and reread the *Mechanics*. And, indeed, it turned out that much of the Mach scholarship (so called) is ideology, not fact, and that it can be exploded by a little relaxed reading of Mach's basic works. Dingler impressed me with his clarity, his confidence, and the way in which he built science from decisions. For years afterward I defused facts with suitably chosen ad hoc hypotheses. At fifteen I also got involved in my first "scientific controversy"— with Johannes Lang, an exponent of the hollow-Earth theory, according to which the Earth is a hollow sphere; the fixed stars are deposits of minerals on a smaller sphere inside. Lang argued from facts (distant plumb lines in mines diverge), mathematical considerations (inversion turns straight lines outside a unit-circle into circles inside, preserving all angles), and bits and pieces of sham history (Neptune was discovered far away from its predicted orbit and was found by sheer accident). I didn't know the motivation for the theory, but there it was, I had read it, and I attacked it in a letter to its author. My main argument was one of simplicity: there are always various ways of connecting and correcting "facts," but the accepted way is the simplest. I also mentioned some mistakes. The reply (I still have it) contains the following sentence: "You are like a mouse trying to make a large building collapse by nibbling at its ornaments."

While this was going on, I sang in a mixed choir under the direction of Leo Lehner, a well-known conductor, composer, and chorus master. Lehner was our music teacher at school. He would often come late, sit down at the piano, and point to one of us, saying, "Get me Steffi [or some other girl] from 6b" (the school had been coeducational, but the girls were gradually being phased out). When Steffi (or Gertrude, or whoever) arrived, Lehner would put his arm around her and start composing. He played the organ during Sunday mass (obligatory at the time) and often enlivened the holy proceedings with popular tunes. A few members of the choir, myself included, were allowed to join him in the organ loft. I sang solos and made quite an impression, for I had a clear, powerful alto voice. The choir appeared at political events; we gave radio concerts (with Josef Holzer, the resident conductor of the radio orchestra, and Max Schönherr, his occasional replacement); we performed in the two large concert halls (Konzerthaussaal, Musikvereinsaal) and, during the Christmas season, on the snow-covered steps of the major downtown churches. I started practicing the violin, and I listened to the radio, which meant, first, a crystal detector set with earphones and, later on, a secondhand tube set. Hearing a particularly interesting song or aria, I would search for the text, learn it, and then sing the piece, day in day out—to the disgust of our neighbors. I had no score and I could not read music; I learned songs, arias, and entire operatic parts, just by listening.

I admired opera, which seemed to be the perfect medium for my grandiose acting style. But it was a long time before I attended a live performance. Having my own rather idiosyncratic views about how the world was arranged, I thought that opera houses and theaters could be entered only by special permission and were inaccessible to teenage mortals like myself. At any rate, the tickets would be far too expensive. I looked at posters and photographs, I identified the names of the singers I knew from the radio, I marveled at the difference between the roles they sang and their private appearance—but I never even thought of going beyond that. Then Lehner was replaced by Johann Langer, a former opera singer. Langer assembled us around the piano; after explaining the basic plots of operas, he performed them, singing all the parts himself. This was the push I needed. I bought a ticket to the Volksoper (to my great surprise I could afford it) and soon became a hopeless addict.

At that time (about 1939 to 1942) the Volksoper had excellent productions with outstanding singers and good conductors. To hear Georg Oeggl as Tonio, Rigoletto, or Beckmesser was a revelation. Oeggl had started in dialect plays. His acting style was simple but highly effective. He had an extraordinary voice—dark, velvety, like the night sky. He sang a lot, occasionally three major roles in a row. I remember a weekend when he sang Luna, Beckmesser, and Rigoletto; he was excellent as Luna, still excellent as Beckmesser ("endlich ein gesungener Beckmesser"—"at last a Beckmesser who sings his part," wrote the critics), but he showed signs of wear as Rigoletto. He started recording when his voice was already in decline. Two parts seemed to have been written especially for him: Tonio and Rigoletto. Nobody moved during "Pari siamo" ("Gleich sind wir beide"—all operas were sung in German), a great piece of music brought to life by a great artist. Members of the Staatsoper occasionally came over—and disappointed us, which means mama and me, for we often went together. I had admired Georg Monthy on the radio, but I found his Rigoletto crude and uninspiring. Alfred Jerger was a legend, but his Hans

Sachs was barely audible. "Is this all the Staatsoper has to offer?" I asked myself, and went to the big house. There I saw a performance of *The Flying Dutchman*, with Hans Hotter in the title role. This was Hotter's first visit to Vienna. He was already famous and I wondered how he would compare with Willy Schwenkreis, another baritone from the Volksoper. "Well?" asked mama when I returned. "Willy Schwenkreis is much better," I said, by which I meant "much louder." Later, after the war, I became aware of Hotter's strength. Here was another unique voice whose best qualities were never captured on record.

Noticing my fascination, Langer invited me to his home and gave me vocal instruction. "You should go to an academy," he said after a few lessons. Papa agreed and prepared the way. I passed the entrance exam and was accepted. I was assigned to an excellent teacher, Adolf Vogel of the State Opera, a famous Leporello, Beckmesser, Alberich, Varlaam, with pupils from all over the world (one of them was Norman Bailey, the mighty Macbeth, the Flying Dutchman, Hans Sachs, and Gremin).

Learning to sing is very different from learning how to think, though there are similarities. One has books for both—the scores of operas, masses, oratorios in the one case; textbooks, papers, lecture notes in the other. You can learn by watching people who excel. But a voice is not a brain. Applied to a task that exceeds its momentary capacity, a brain becomes baffled, does not understand, but remains in good working order (I am speaking of mathematical or physical problems, not of the thought that goes into a play or a novel). A voice used in a similar situation falters, weakens, and disappears. Hundreds of talented artists have lost their voices singing parts that were too difficult for their capacities or for their stage of development. A mathematical genius, while requiring some training, can start right away with the most complicated problems. There is no need to "grow." A singer must wait. At twenty, he or she cannot sing something that demands ten years of physical, musical, and spiritual preparation. The reason is that singing involves the entire body, not just the lungs, the brain, and the diaphragm. Just enter a conservatory and listen: here, a few bars of a cello concerto; over there, scales produced by an uncertain voice; a piano intervenes; an aria is heard in the distance, clear, well phrased, but it is interrupted because of a minor error in intonation. Everywhere minds and bodies and souls are invited, begged, cajoled, ordered to merge and to attend to the work at hand.

And there are almost as many methods as there are teachers. Some teachers use songs and arias right away. They choose a simple piece of music that requires only a rudimentary vocal ability and try to build the voice by working on it. After a while they move on to the next piece, experimenting as they go along. Others start with scales, proceed to vocal exercises, and finally arrive at arias that require no particular vocal category. The category (tenor or baritone, basso cantante or basso profundo), they believe, will emerge in the course of the training. Still others stay with scales for months, even years. A teacher may interfere with the personal life of a pupil; for example, he may advise a virgin soprano to get laid in order to add some sparkle to her voice. (Today the advice is hardly needed, but it was when I started singing, and some teachers did the needed work themselves.) There are teachers who get carried away by a beautiful voice and encourage their pupils to sing music far beyond them. Others are strict and conservative.

Vogel belonged to the latter category. He asked me to talk softly and under no circumstances to try anything operatic. I sang scales, pianissimo, piano, mezzoforte at the very most. We encountered difficulties. I got hoarse, produced an astounding variety of ugly sounds; but slowly Vogel and I succeeded in placing my voice. It changed character and grew until my mouth seemed much too small to contain it. "This is a world voice," people said when, disregarding Vogel's advice, I tried an aria or a Lied; I was even approached by a theatrical agent who heard me performing on a streetcar.

The course of my life was now clear: theoretical astronomy during the day, preferably in the domain of perturbation theory; then rehearsals, coaching, vocal exercises, opera in the evening (buffoons like van Bett or bastards like Scarpia); and astronomical observation at night. A picture I painted during this time shows one side of my plan. There I am, high up on an inaccessible mountain, peering through a telescope at an immaculate sky. The only remaining obstacle was the war. "All that hard work will have been in vain," said Vogel when I got my draft notice. He was right.

4 Occupation and War

In March 1938, Austria became part of Germany. For some people—a small minority—Anschluss was the end of civilized life. For others it meant being liberated from the tyranny of a Catholic totalitarianism that had ruled Austria for years. Still others welcomed unification with the Big Brother and the increase in power it implied. "Look at our planes!" they exclaimed when the German air force circled over Vienna. There were rumors of progress, of an end to stagnation, of great opportunities. "We shall soon be working again," said the unemployed; "They are going to take care of us," said the destitute; "At last we are free," said the politically disadvantaged, prominent socialists among them. Adolf Hitler played an important and, considering the way he is being portrayed today, rather amazing role in this process.

Many Austrians had followed his rise to power in Germany and had heard him on the radio. These were well-choreographed events. A popular announcer described the location, the size of the audience, the political and cultural leaders present, and the networks that would carry the speech. It was a long list; during the war and to some extent even before the war, many foreign stations were also involved. Military bands played familiar tunes. They stopped, started, stopped, started again—Hitler was never punctual. Suddenly the Badenweilermarsch, Hitler's favorite. Enthusiastic shouting was heard in the distance, came nearer, grew in volume until the entire audience was a single roaring voice exulting with joy. One or two speeches by Goebbels, Hess, Göring, or some local Nazi bosses and then, finally, Hitler. He would begin slowly, hesitantly, in a low but resonant voice: "Volksgenossen und Volksgenossinnen!"—"Fellow nationals, men and women!" Many people, young and old, male and female, my mother among them, were hypnotized by his voice. Listening to the mere sound they became transfixed. "I loved Hitler," Ingmar Bergman writes in his autobiography, reporting his impressions as an adolescent exchange student. "The only face among faceless men," was Heidegger's reaction. "He is a phenomenon—too bad I am a Jew and he is an anti-Semite," said Josef von Sternberg, inventor of Marlene Dietrich, director of *The Blue Angel* and many Hollywood movies afterward. Hitler mentioned local problems and achievements; he made jokes, some of them rather good. Gradually his delivery changed; in approaching obstacles and setbacks, Hitler increased both his speed and his volume. The outbursts, which are the only parts of his speeches known the world over, were carefully prepared, well staged, and exploited in a calmer vein once they had passed. They were the result of control, not of anger, hatred, or despair, at least while Hitler was still in good physical shape and in command of events. "Here is a man who knows how to speak," said papa, who had been looking forward to the takeover, "not like Schuschnigg" (the Austrian chancellor, an intellectual without temperament or popular appeal). How did these events affect me? What were my impressions? What did I do?

In the summer of 1988 I read François Jacob's autobiography, *The Statue Within.* Jacob tells how, as a young man, he had decided to leave France and to fight Hitler despite the truce and the existence of a "neutral" France under Pétain. Jacob had a clear view of the situation; he had strong feelings about right and wrong and he acted accordingly. My perception was different. Much of what happened I learned only after the war, from articles, books, and television, and the events I did notice either made no impression at all or affected me in a random way. I remember them and I can describe them, but there was no context to give them meaning and no aim to judge them by.

On March 14, 1938 (or was it March 15?), the day Hitler entered Vienna, I started on my usual walk toward the center of town. I didn't get very far. Some streets were closed by the police, others were jammed with enthusiastic spectators. A religious mania seemed to engulf the place. Thoroughly annoyed, I returned home. There my father listened to the announcements on the radio; I tried to stop him—the noise interfered with my reading. (This was an old battle: papa thrived on the news; I couldn't have cared less about it.) For me the German occupation and the war that followed were an inconvenience, not a moral problem, and my reactions came from accidental moods and circumstances, not from a well-defined outlook.

So I praised the British when mama, defending the popular line, condemned them. We had a big fight. But I also wrote, produced, and performed in a farce caricaturing the situation in the House of Commons (I played Chamberlain with his umbrella; I was fifteen at the time). I left a gathering of the Hitler Youth with the remark—which was received with astonishment, derision, and some anger—that I had to attend Holy Mass (it was not true; I just chose the most outrageous excuse I could think of). On other occasions I obeyed orders; for example, I went to the homes of absentees to bring them to the meetings (I did not always succeed; some parents simply threw me out). When papa bought *Mein Kampf,* I read it aloud to the assembled family. "What a ridiculous way of making a point," I thought, "crude, repetitive, more barking than speech." Yet I concluded an essay on Goethe (a school assignment) by linking him to Hitler. There was no insight behind this maneuver, no deeply felt conviction; the desire for a good grade certainly played no role; nor had I fallen for Hitler's "cha-

risma," as had artists, philosophers, scientists, and millions of ordinary men and women. So what made me do it? I assume it was
the tendency (still with me) to pick up strange views and push
them to the extreme. I was greatly moved by the first few pages of
Rosenberg's *Mythos des Zwanzigsten Jahrhunderts* (Myth of the
twentieth century); I almost felt the flow of the national blood
and the power of the Whole from which it sprang. Two years later,
during the collective oath that completed my induction into the
working service (*Arbeitsdienst*), I tried to revive the emotion; I did
not succeed. I concluded that it had been a fluke and that the oath
was without content.

At the end of our training in Germany the company commander offered a choice: we could go to France as part of the occupation force or stay behind and keep the barracks clean. I raised
my hand: "I want to stay right here." The commander came toward me. "Why?" he asked. "Because I want to read without being
disturbed." "People like you ought to be eradicated [*ausgerottet*],"
he said, and denied my request. I can still see the consuming hatred on his face. (In France I tried to lie my way out of it; I was
caught and assigned to an especially nasty unit.) Yet when stuck
on the shores of Lake Peipus I grew bored and asked to be sent to
where the fighting was. "You are much too valuable to be wasted
now," said Herr von Bewersdorff; "we'll need you after the war."

Around that time I also considered joining the SS. Why? Because an SS man looked better and spoke better and walked better
than ordinary mortals; aesthetics, not ideology, was my reason. (I
remember feeling a strong erotic undercurrent while discussing
the matter with a fellow soldier.) During battle I often forgot to
take cover. It was not out of bravery—I am a great coward and easily frightened—but out of excitement: flames on the horizon,
shooting, indistinct voices, attacks from planes in the air and
tanks on the ground—it was like a theater and I acted accordingly.
On one such occasion I got the Iron Cross, on another three

bullets—one in my face, one in my right hand, the third in my spine. While still at school I told our music teacher that I had seen Stravinsky's picture in a shop window. Stravinsky, I thought, was a Jew, and exhibiting his picture was in violation of the existing laws. (In fact, Stravinsky was not a Jew; he was an anti-Semite, but few people knew that.) I felt no sense of outrage, needed no favors, and was not in any trouble; I just wanted to establish some personal contact. (This need often made me act in a somewhat servile way.)

Yet on other occasions I ridiculed the ideas of bodily excellence, military valor, or the then popular identification of fascism with ancient Rome. "What's the difference between strong muscles and a big belly?" I asked our German teacher (who was also our chief ideologist) in front of the class. "A stupid person isn't helped by either." "Why be courageous?" I continued. "A wise man runs when things get dangerous." I criticized an Italian movie that likened Mussolini to Julius Caesar (or Augustus—I don't remember which). "What a farce!" I said; "modern Italy isn't even a shadow of ancient Rome!" Dr. Baaz, our new and politically correct director who had just entered the classroom, was not amused. "Where did you see that movie?" he inquired. "I haven't seen it," I replied. "It was a propaganda movie. If I'd seen it I would have been taken in and couldn't have given an objective report." I must have been very proud of that reply to remember it to this day.

Looking back, I notice a rather unstable combination of contrariness and a tendency to conform. A critical judgment or a feeling of unease could be silenced or turned into its opposite by an almost imperceptible counterforce. It was like a fragile cloud dispersed by heat. On other occasions I would not listen to reason or Nazi common sense and would cling to unpopular ideas. This ambivalence (which survived for many years and has weakened only recently) seems to have been connected with my ambivalence toward people: I wanted to be close to them, but I also wanted to be left alone.

The change of government was followed by changes at school. Some teachers disappeared, others were transferred. "He is a Jew," or "He has a Jewish wife," we said, without paying much attention; this, at least, is how it appears to me today, in retrospect. Then the Jewish members of our class were assigned a special bench at the back of the classroom. There were three of them, Weinberg, Altendorf, and Neuern. Neuern had blue-green eyes and curly hair; he sat in the first row, on the right-hand side, next to Hlavka, whom I admired; Altendorf was fat and had a whining voice; Weinberg had brown eyes, was graceful and well dressed. I can see them now, as if they had left only yesterday. We were instructed to keep our distance, and most of us complied, though halfheartedly. I remember circling Weinberg in the yard during a break and moving away again. Then they, too, disappeared. People wearing yellow stars appeared on buses and trams and in the streets; Jewish colleagues visited my father and asked for advice; our old family doctor, Dr. Kronfeld, a genial and jocular gentleman, could no longer practice and was replaced by Dr. Fischer, another genial and jocular gentleman; one of our neighbors, Herr Kopstein, and his son left the block, pushing a cart with their belongings—"They are going away," said papa. All these events were as strange and distant as the jugglers and street singers of earlier times, the shelling of the workers' quarters in 1934, the dead bodies and the bloody sidewalks I ran into when returning from school, the sexual assault on me when I was thirteen—and just as opaque. It never occurred to me to inquire further; the idea that the fate of every single human being was in some way connected with my own existence was entirely outside my field of vision.

In April 1942, four weeks after I had passed my final high school exams (the *Matura*), I was drafted into the *Arbeitsdienst* and sent to Pirmasens for basic training. I and the two other Austrians in our company soon became unpopular; we were lazy and more than ready to leave responsibilities to those who constantly talked about them. The authorities restored order by assigning us to different units. My unit ended up in Quelerne en Bas, near Brest, in Brittany. It was a monotonous life. During the week we moved around in the countryside, dug ditches, and filled them up again. On weekends everybody went to Brest for sex and booze. The ladies were quite forthcoming—"They go straight for your fly," a guy from the advance commando said with awe in his voice. I stayed home. This was partly an act ("I'm a special person who doesn't do silly things like that"), partly laziness. The camp was empty and quiet, nobody gave any orders, and I could sleep or read the books I had brought with me. Since my attitude pleased neither the men nor the officers, they decided to teach me a lesson. Two parties formed; one wanted to beat me up, the other was for leaving me alone. Eventually there was a big fight; not I, but my defenders and detractors, got bloody noses. I was thrown into prison once—I have forgotten why—and I often had to do extra duty. I remember fragments and moods: the toilet on the hill behind the barracks, the drunken excesses of the staff, an excursion to Brest, the songs on the radio which wove a melancholy veil around everything. Most of the political and military events passed me by without leaving an impression. I had noticed the war against Poland and France. The invasion of Russia could hardly be overlooked—daily reports were introduced by the main theme from Liszt's *Les Préludes*. I was vaguely aware of what happened during the winter of 1941–42. Later on I met soldiers who wore the *Gefrierfleischorden*, the frozen meat medal, which they received for having survived without winter clothes. I never heard of Pearl Harbor, and most of the events of 1942–-44 did not register; I simply was not interested. My stay in Brest ended in November and I returned home. My parents were surprised at the habits and speech patterns I had acquired; I was surprised at the smallness of our apartment. Two weeks before Christmas I left again, this time for the army.

Training ensued at Reserve Engineer Battalion 86 in Krems, near Vienna. After a few weeks I volunteered for officers' school. I had no urge for leadership, only a wish to survive: the candidates received additional instruction on safe places—perhaps the war would be over before we were sent to the front. Our first location was Sisak, Yugoslavia. We lived at a high school near the center of town and worked on the banks of the river Sava. There we learned to dismantle and clean guns, to lay and discover mines, to construct and destroy bridges, to build, detect, and defuse bombs, and other useful things. Assembling units of pontoon bridges was our least favorite occupation. The parts, all prefabricated, were laid out in the sand; eight soldiers (I believe) stood at attention in front of them. A brief command, and the exercise began. Groups of two or four performed carefully standardized actions. People stumbled, fell into the water, collapsed under a heavy piece of equipment—and had to start all over again. I was ordered to the hospital twice because my hands had become bleeding sores. I had a sunny room, read Keller's *Grüner Heinrich,* and decided to become a painter.

Next we moved to Vukovar. It was there that I learned of mama's suicide. I was sitting in the common room trying to devise a simple and convincing diagram of the Lorentz transformations. One of my friends approached: "Can I talk to you alone?" We went to an open window in the corridor. It was dark; one could hardly see the garden or the trees. He told me. I thanked him and went back to my sketches. I felt absolutely nothing. The rest of the group already knew; they had debated how to inform me in the gentlest possible way. They were astounded, even appalled at my behavior; and they said so when I returned from Vienna.

Mama had died on July 29, 1943. I arrived on August 4; the burial took place August 5. Mama's body rested on an elevated structure, slightly above our heads. Her mouth had collapsed and her lips were black. Papa wanted to take a closer look; I pulled him back: "Don't look at her now," I said; "Try to remember her as she was when she lived." The body was transferred to the coffin, the coffin lowered into the grave, and we started throwing earth on it. I lost my shovel, which fell on the coffin with a bang. And then I had a big surprise. I thought that Father Egger, the priest from our nearby church, would conduct the funeral. Father Brandmeier, my religious instructor from high school, a kind man and a masterful orator, turned up instead. I suspect that Egger had refused to bury a suicide, that papa had turned to Brandmeier for help, and that Brandmeier had found a way. Again people commented on how cold and unmoved I looked throughout the ceremony.

Aunt Julie, not my favorite relative, now ran the household. Uncle Rudolf paid a visit: "What did you do to her?" Papa and I went on long walks and talked about trivial things. Back in Yugoslavia I wrote my impressions on the cover of a copy of Goethe's *Iphigenie*. It was a sunny day and I was sitting in a cornfield. I wrote about my father's sorrow, about our separation, the war, and the uncertainty of life. I had the "right" thoughts and considered the "right" things—but my emotions were twisted and shallow, more paper dramatics than genuine feeling. I was aware of the discrepancy although I had no examples to guide me. Slowly the impressions faded; what remained were the day-to-day problems of life in an occupied country.

We never ran into the Resistance and rarely thought of ourselves as an occupying force. From Vukovar we moved to Brod, Banja Luki, Novi Sad, Vincovci, and back again. During one of these trips a fellow soldier and I went through a field toward a

OCCUPATION AND WAR **45**

farmhouse. An old woman appeared at the gate. We were hungry, and asked, in German, for milk and cornbread. The woman answered in English—she had been in the United States and still had relatives there. She was kind, civil; she talked with us at length but gave us no food. She explained why: we were the enemy. That really surprised us. In November we had a brief vacation; on December 11, 1943, we were finally sent into battle.

Again I remember only isolated episodes. I can locate some of them, but I have no idea where and when the rest occurred. Until about five years ago I thought I had been in Kiev; a little checking back and forth convinced me that I never left the northern part of the Russian front. It didn't really matter—life was unpleasant everywhere. We were deposited near Staraja Russa; we ended up on the western shore of Lake Peipus, near Pskov. I was advanced to lance corporal (*Gefreiter*) in October 1943, to sergeant (*Unteroffizier*) and candidate for lieutenant in April '44, and to lieutenant toward the end of that year—this is what my army records say; my mind, however, is a blank.

Our first quarters were holes in the ground with wooden bunks for beds. The earth was hard when we arrived; it soon turned into mud. Mud was everywhere; reddish-brown mud; on our boots, in our faces, on our hands, on our shirts, in our hair. We didn't walk, we slid around. On the day of our arrival a soldier shot himself trying to dismantle a pistol. He stood there with a puzzled look as blood left his body in a perfect parabola. The parabola rose and fell, shrank, and finally disappeared. For a few weeks we simply waited; we ate, slept, cleaned our guns, and watched the horizon. Then the retreat began.

Marching across the countryside we blew up every house we found; we put charges in strategic places, lit the fuse, and ran. We slept on the ovens, with rifle, gas mask, tornister, dagger, munition right beside us. The ovens were still warm; the inhabitants had left only a few hours earlier. We heard artillery and saw fires, but we never saw a single Russian soldier. There were no civilians either—with two exceptions. On one occasion a huge infantry-man I had noticed before herded civilians, men and women, into a cellar about two hundred meters from where I was standing, and threw a hand grenade after them. "What did he do that for?" my neighbor asked. On another occasion a small, mean-looking individual shot a civilian right in the head. These events did not shock me—they were too strange for that; yet they have stayed with me, and they make me shiver when I think of them today.

We stopped briefly to celebrate Christmas. I composed a sketch and sang a ballad describing the fate of wise old Socrates. I am surprised to read that I earned the Iron Cross early in March 1944—I thought it was much later. This is what happened. Lying in the snow, we were attacked by planes—a rarity in Russia—and from the ground by gunfire. We were afraid—I know I was—and tried to disappear into the ground. Our tanks rolled back and forth. They crushed one of our soldiers. He lay there, flat, like a piece of cardboard. We moved on. It grew dark. As we approached a village, we were shot at. I grabbed a manual rocket launcher, a *Panzerfaust,* jumped onto a slightly elevated road, ran toward the village, and encouraged others to follow me. We entered the village and occupied it for a few hours; then we were on the run again. I mention the incident as an example not of my courage but of my idiocy, and to illustrate the way my memory works. At any rate, I was awarded an Iron Cross, second class. I lost it long ago, but I still have the confirmation, right here in my *Soldbuch.*

Sometime during that year, either before or after the events I have just mentioned, I was put in command of a company of seasoned soldiers. There I was, a dedicated bookworm, with no experience, the symbols of authority on my shoulders, confronted with a bunch of skeptical experts. It happened to me again, twenty years later, when I was supposed to teach the Indians, blacks, and Hispanics who had entered the university as part of Lyndon Johnson's educational programs. Who was I to tell these people what to think? And who was I, in 1944, to give orders to men who had been in the war for years? I started making conversation—rumors I had heard about troop movements—just to establish some kind of contact. I failed. We moved west and eventually arrived at Lake Peipus. There was little to do; some shooting during the day, colorful flares during the night. Occasionally an officer sent a unit across the lake, but most of the time the soldiers simply stood in their holes, watching the horizon and waiting for the replacement. The weather was beautiful, one sunny day after another; it almost felt like vacation time at a national park. I took long walks and began to practice my singing again. During the night I checked the observation posts. I called out the password, jumped into the hole, explained the constellations and peculiar stars, added relevant astrophysical information, and moved on to the next hole. Weeks later some of "my men" told me, "You're crazy, but you're OK. But when you arrived, well, we thought you were a real asshole!"

Having completed my assignment I returned, along with the other candidates, to the officers' school at Dessau Rosslau, a little town about fifty kilometers from Leipzig. Now we studied tactics, the history of warfare, military law, explosives, guns, etc. and went off to training exercises. I organized the farewell show with versified mockery for everyone. I also gave a series of lectures. I don't know how that came about, but I can still see the instructors sitting in front of me with partly skeptical, partly irritated expressions on their faces. I still have the complete text of the lectures—forty pages of a six-by-eight-inch notebook. This is truly miraculous, for I am not in the habit of assembling memorabilia. I began the course November 21, 1944, and ended December 1. Here is the beginning of the second lecture, written in the bloated style I used at the time.

"Before I continue with my remarks," I said, "I want to deal with events that have occurred as a result of my previous lecture. I have a certain well-defined position. I have no intention of being deflected from it by any utterance made by anybody in this room, the reason being that for me my position is unconditionally true. My talk will therefore have a definitive and absolute character. May everybody take from it what he deserves. I don't name names, and nobody who has a good conscience needs to feel offended." This was directed at my fellow soldiers, but it was also directed at the instructors who had ridiculed me for being *lebensfremd,* a stranger to life. "What do you mean by 'life'?" I asked. "If I were to follow you, I would waste my time visiting places that are nothing but overgrown villages and discussing wind and weather in the company of mindless women. Is that what you philistines mean by 'life'?" The true connection between things, I said, "reveals itself to the solitary thinker and not to people who are fascinated by noise." People have different professions, different points of view. They are like observers looking at the world through the narrow windows of an otherwise closed structure. Occasionally they assemble at the center and discuss what they have seen; "then one observer will talk about a beautiful landscape with red trees, a red sky, and a red lake in the middle; the next one about an infinite blue plane without articulation, and the third about an impressive, five-floor-high building; they will quarrel. The observer on top of their structure [me] can only laugh at their quarrels—but for them the quarrels will be real and he will be an unworldly dreamer." Real life, I said, is exactly like that. "Every person has his own well-defined opinions, which color the section of the world he perceives. And when people come together, when they try to discover the nature of the whole to which they belong, they are bound to talk past each other; they will understand neither themselves nor their companions. I have often experienced, painfully, this impenetrability of human beings—whatever happens, whatever is said, rebounds from the smooth surface that separates them from each other."

My main thesis was that historical periods such as the Baroque, the Rococo, the Gothic Age are unified by a concealed essence that only a lonely outsider can understand. Most people see only the obvious. For example, they quote Arndt, Koerner, and Schenkendorf to illustrate the spirit of the wars of liberation (again Napoleon). This, I said, is very naive. We can admit that times of war produce warlike writers—but that does not exhaust their nature. One must also study those who were untouched by the patriotic fervor and were perhaps averse to it; they too represent their age (I took as an example the many interests of the later Goethe). Secondly, I said, it is a mistake to assume that the essence of a historical period that started in one place can be transferred to another. There will be influences, true; for example, the French Enlightenment influenced Germany. But the trends arising from the influence share only the name with their cause. Finally, it is a mistake to evaluate events by comparing them with an ideal. Many writers have deplored the way in which the Catholic Church transformed Good Germans during the Middle Ages and later and forced them into actions and beliefs unnatural to them. Now "unnatural" actions do not come from the center of a person or a group; they come from the mind, which creates aggregates, not harmonic wholes. Being a purely formal agency, it works by analysis and recombination. But Gothic art produced harmonic units, not aggregates. This shows that the forms of the Church were not alien forms (*artfremd,* a favorite term at the time), and the Germans of that period were natural Christians, not unwilling and cowardly slaves. I concluded by applying the lesson to the relations between Germans and Jews. Jews, I said, are supposed to be aliens, miles removed from genuine Germans; they are supposed to have distorted the German character and to have changed the German nation into a collection of pessimistic, egotistical, mate-

rialistic individuals. But, I continued, the Germans reached that
stage all by themselves. They were ready for liberalism and even
Marxism. "Everybody knows how the Jew, who is a fine psycholo-
gist, made use of this situation. What I mean is that the soil for his
work was well prepared. Our misfortune is our own work, and
we must not put the blame on any Jew, or Frenchman or En-
glishman."

After training I went home for Christmas, back to Krems to receive
new equipment, and then again to the front. On January 2, 1945, I
wrote (in the notebook from which I have just quoted): "Second-
to-last day of my leave. Tomorrow we are off to be reunited with
the restless confusion that is the war. How long is it going to last?
What remains are the memories: of my books, of my father, of all
the things I have come to love and which now cling to me and
cause me pain . . . How easy it was to mock tradition as a concern
for things that long ago outlived themselves! Wasn't it I who
preached: Forget your parents! Forget the bonds of family—they
will only hinder you; think of yourself, of your aims, and try to
realize them—and now that I am about to leave I cannot stop embracing my father, and even the smallest object from his hand
moves me to tears. And what about my books? Every day I am
afraid to lose them, and I don't know how I shall feel if the enemy
lays hand on them . . . One must learn to renounce simple plea-
sures, and the war is a great teacher in this respect. The war reveals
the essence of a person—many irrelevant things disappear . . ."
and so on. Boy! What a strange mixture of genuine feelings and
empty talk. I can see a bit of Nietzsche in it too—I had read
Zarathustra and had fallen for the bombast contained in that
work. On January 3 we boarded the train for the front. We sat, ate,
and slept in cattle wagons with traces of straw on the floor. One
night I woke up with a strange sensation around my midriff: I had

wet my pants. I undressed, dried my underwear, and went back to sleep.

Our destination was Poland, the area near Czestochowa. There I was put in command of a bicycle company. I was hardly thrilled—I had never ridden a bicycle, and I fell off when I tried. The soldiers stood around looking puzzled: this is supposed to be our leader? The problem was solved by the Russians; in one day the bicycles were already in their hands. And then came two weeks of absolute chaos. Run, rest, build a bridge, cross the bridge, blow up the bridge, remove mines, lay mines, rest, run again. I remember sitting in a house, reading a book, with anxious peasants around me; soaking my feet in warm water when the Russians entered by the back door—I still don't know how I escaped; sleeping in a barn and seeing the Russians through a small crack when I opened my eyes in the morning; running across a field to escape gunfire, with people dropping like flies around me.

One by one the higher-ups disappeared. The first lieutenant, an unsympathetic fellow with a frozen smirk on his face, held up his little finger; there was blood on it. "I have to move ahead to the hospital," he said; "You take over." Next came the captain; then the major. After a few days I was in command of three tanks; an infantry battalion; auxiliary troops from Finland, Poland, the Ukraine; and masses of German refugees. There was not much to do as the task was clear: go west, and as quickly as possible. People were overjoyed when we entered a village that had been occupied, but we didn't stop; we drove right through and saw their faces disappear in the distance. More civilians, first from Poland, then from what soon became East Germany, joined us: rumor had it that the Russians were cruel victors. At one point we hid behind an extended ridge. Soldiers were moving around in a village we had just left. Russians. People like us—but monstrously distorted by fear and propaganda. They left the village and advanced. We shot at them, halfheartedly. They continued. A man rose. "Down!" I shouted. He got up again and ran. Others followed. I joined, urging everybody to stay together.

Then, one evening, in the midst of shooting from right, left, front, back, the horizon aflame with burning houses, my carelessness finally caught up with me. Playing the operatic hero once again, I placed myself at a crossroad and started directing traffic. Suddenly my face was burning. I touched my cheek. Blood. Next, an impact on my right hand. I looked at it. There was a large hole in my glove. I didn't like that at all. The gloves were made of excellent leather and lined with fur; I would have liked them to remain intact. I turned slightly to the left—things were getting dangerous. I slipped and fell. I tried to get up but I couldn't. I felt no pain, but I was convinced that my legs had been shattered. For a moment I saw myself in a wheelchair, moving along endless shelves of books—I was almost happy. Soldiers eager to get out of trouble gathered around me, lifted me onto a sledge, and dragged me away. The war was over as far as I was concerned.

Years later, these events turned up in my dreams, though in a strangely transformed way. I did not and still do not dream about battle scenes and dangerous encounters. I dream about my induction into the army. The situation is always the same. I get the draft notice. "Ah," I say, "I don't have to go, I'm a cripple" (which I am—I have been on crutches since 1946). I enter the barracks, get into line, and then—lo and behold!—I can walk. "What a lousy joke," I think. "There I was, dragging myself around for years, but now that I don't need it my legs suddenly work." Alternatively, I remember (all this in the dream) that I am a lieutenant. "I'm an officer," I say to myself. "I won't have to take part in the exercises." But nobody notices my uniform, and I have to stand in line like everybody else. Another dream is about the wake-up calls and the preparations for the day. I open my eyes; I'm in the barracks; I know I have to be ready, washed, dressed, fed in a very short time. I have trouble getting into the bathroom—many people are in my way. I try to shave but can't find my razor. I want to eat, but I'm late and don't know where to go. The showers are occupied, the toilets dirty—"I'll never make it," I say to myself. In fact, I never did have problems of that sort; I was fast and often had time left for a little reading. I don't remember being apprehensive either—so where does all this commotion come from?

I often dream of having committed treason or murder. Occasionally I have a bundle containing the disfigured remnants of my victim. I know that my days are counted—Will I be discovered? Will I be executed? In some dreams I remain free, but without hope and without any future to speak of. On other occasions I am arrested and led to the gallows. "This time it can't be a dream, this time it's real," I say to myself—and wake up. I don't think these dreams have anything to do with the war; the murders are individual murders and the treason is of an unspecified kind. Once I even strangled myself, lying on a bed in front of me, and then sniffed at the dead body for signs of putrefaction.

During the Nazi period I paid little attention to the general talk about Jews, communism, the Bolshevik threat; I did not accept it, I did not oppose it; the words came and went, apparently without effect. Years later I had many Jewish friends, in the United States, in England, on the European Continent; as a matter of fact, almost all the friends I have made in my profession are Jews, according to the Nazi definition. I didn't know that when our friendship started. When I found out, mostly by accident, I felt that something rather special was happening. "He is a Jew, and he is a good friend of mine"—it was like eating forbidden fruit. The feeling remained for a few years; it has gone away now. In a way I regret it. Feeling differently about different faces, groups, communities seems to be more humane than a humanitarianism that evens out all individual and group idiosyncrasies.

5   Apolda and Weimar

An ambulance brought me to the field hospital. I was undressed and put on an operating table. My legs were in perfect order—not a scratch on them. "It was a bullet," the doctors said, and showed me where it had entered; a tiny hole on my right side, in the lumbar region. "You are paralyzed," they continued; "we have to open you up to see what further damage there is." They made a ten-centimeter-long slit in my belly from the navel downward, searched a little, stitched me up again, and put me on a train. I felt vague pain and had trouble breathing. The officers who had left me behind passed by with a cheerful look on their faces and small bandages on their bodies. They were all there, the first lieutenant, the captain, the major. "What happened to you?" they asked—and were not seen again. I spent a few days at a hospital in Karlsbad. I slept most of the time. Once, during the night, I woke up and saw a beautiful face bending over me. "Do you want some tea?" the apparition asked. "Stay with me," I replied, and fell asleep again. Another train. Finally the central hospital in Weimar.

I soon recovered but remained paralyzed from the waist down. I was not unduly concerned. I even got alarmed when one of my toes started moving; "Not now, please," I said; "can't you wait until the war's over?" I didn't mind being a cripple—I was content; talked to my neighbors; read novels, poems, crime stories, essays of all kinds. Schopenhauer gave me a shock: his description of people who mindlessly stuff themselves with reading matter seemed to fit me perfectly. I heard a radio program on Orson Welles's famous broadcast and its aftereffects. Silly people like that, the commentator said, cannot possibly endanger Germany. During the night we heard bombers on the way to their targets. It was an uncomfortable feeling. They were directly overhead—would they drop their bombs? Would they leave us alone? Then Weimar itself was attacked. The aides carried the patients into the cellar, and even further, into the sewers. My neighbor and I decided to stay where we were. Our courage faded when the windowframe landed on our heads. We couldn't move, and shouted our heads off. It was a long time before we were discovered and taken away. We stayed in the sewers for almost a week; there was little food, no light, and water everywhere. Yet in the midst of the confusion the chief librarian, a determined woman with a stern face and a soft voice, started to collect her books. Eventually some of us were moved to Apolda, a little town near Weimar.

It was there that I heard of Germany's surrender. I was sitting in a wheelchair, in the garden. I was relieved, but I also had a sense of loss. I had not accepted the aims of Nazism—I hardly knew what they were—and I was much too contrary to be loyal to anything. Nor did I feel betrayed, or misused, as did many Vietnam veterans. After I'd been a few weeks in the hospital, the past had almost disappeared. I remembered some of the more dramatic events, but found it hard to believe that I had been part of them. So where did this sense of loss come from? I don't know. What I do know is that great hopes, misplaced efforts, tremendous sacrifices were soon regarded with hatred and contempt. But were not hatred, contempt, and a desire for justice the right attitude toward ideas and actions that had caused and prolonged an atrocious war and led to the murder of millions of innocent people? Of course they were—but the trouble is that the distribution of good and evil is not easy to figure out, at least not for me. Compassion, unselfishness, love can be found in the very center of evil. I don't understand why this should be so, I am only sure of the fact. But if that's how the world is built, then a clear moral vision implies simplifications and, with them, acts of cruelty and injustice.

Slowly I started moving around. First in a wheelchair. At that time wheelchairs had three wheels, one in front, the others behind the seat; the chairs were propelled by levers and could acquire great speed. Pedestrians scattered in terror when I approached. Then came crutches. I put them ahead of me, leaned on them and dragged my body along. I must have had great strength, for I went to movies and plays and went on dates with the resident nurses.

I also had my first real love affair. I had embraced girls before and had even kissed them, but I had never made love, neither before the war, when I was buried in books, nor as a soldier, when I used my free time to rest or to read. I had only the vaguest idea of the geography behind a skirt or a bra—at twenty-one I was still a virgin, and a very ignorant one. (While at high school I had thought that looking at a girl too admiringly would make her pregnant.) World Literature came to my rescue: I read Zola's *Rougon Macquard*. There is a seduction scene; the woman sits on a pile of hay, the man stands in front of her. He kneels down and moves his hand up her thigh. She gets excited. Well, I said; let's see if that works. On the next date my favorite nurse and I went to the local park, sat down on a bench, talked, and kissed as we had before. Slowly I moved my hand up her thigh, and she did indeed get excited. All that was not as calculated as it sounds. What I had read quickly ceased to be information and became habit. About half a year later, when I was already living in Weimar, Rosemarie paid me a visit. We talked, and eventually went to bed—another first. I was embarrassed. I continued reading a cultural journal and talked endlessly about Kant's three critiques. Rosemarie undressed, rose, and stood before me. At last the parts of the puzzle united into an amazing whole: so this was how a woman looked! Needless to say, I was in no position to do what a man is supposed to do in such circumstances. I soon realized that I would never be; the bullet that got me out of the war had made me impotent.

I was healthy and mobile, but without an occupation. I went to the mayor of Apolda, a worker and an antifascist who had just returned from Russia. I explained my situation and asked for a job—paid, unpaid, it didn't matter. Thinking back, I am amazed at my actions and at the mayor's response. After all, I was a former officer of the government that had expelled him. Yet he showed neither surprise nor hatred; he did not even inquire if I had been a member of the Nazi party. He simply gave me an office and a secretary, and assigned me to the education section. Entertainment was my business. I wrote speeches, dialogues, sketches for various occasions; I rehearsed them and supervised the final performance. I also wrote a play with small parts for children from the local kindergarten and larger parts for artists from the Nationaltheater Weimar, but I fell ill during rehearsals and had to go back to bed. I might have become a good director, perhaps a great one; I enjoyed what I was doing and was much too ignorant to have scruples or be nervous.

When I recovered, I went to the music academy in Weimar to continue with my studies. I auditioned with Maxim Vallentin, Josef Maria Hauschild, and, after that, the entire staff. Maxim Vallentin, the former director of the German Theater in Moscow, was a leading proponent of the Stanislavski method. Hauschild was a well-known lieder singer, somewhat conceited ("I can sing the entire *Winterreise* without an interval"), but kind and considerate. I was accepted, awarded a scholarship, received food stamps (I was classified *Schwerarbeiter*, heavy worker), and started my "heavy work." I was still living at the hospital in Apolda and commuted to Weimar by train. To finance the enterprise I sold my army watches to Russian soldiers—in three steps: first some money and a less valuable watch; then more money and a still less valuable watch; finally a public show to get a good price for the last watch. I rubbed it with lard, immersed it in water, pointed out that it was still working, and accepted the largest offer. Total result: two thousand marks—a huge sum at the time.

After about three months I moved to Weimar. I found a basement in which a salesman had put a metal bed amid some abandoned stoves and furnaces. It was a large, cold room with a single bulb hanging from a wire, water running down the walls, a small window showing the feet of passing pedestrians, and spiders and cockroaches to keep me company. Here I slept, read (Kierkegaard, Devrient's history of the theater, Thomas Mann, whose *Joseph in Egypt* had just appeared), made notes, and received visitors. I also discovered a way of attending rehearsals and performances at the Nationaltheater. Going in by a side entrance, I walked along a corridor reserved for actors and took a seat in the box of the Soviet City Commander. Nobody challenged me, not even the general himself, who occasionally appeared with his staff.

I saw drama (I remember Hebbel's *Maria Magdalena*), operas, ballet; and listened to concerts. *Fidelio* disappointed me. Too much shouting; too much gesticulating; too many Good People. "That doesn't surprise me," Rosemarie said; "you've been in a war. But wait, your love for the stage will return." This was the time when well-known artists turned up in unexpected places. Peter Anders gave a recital; Heinrich Kraayvanger, a tenor of the Vienna State Opera, sang in *Pagliacci,* in *Land des Lächelns,* and in a concert. "He's going to scream like a pig," I said to Rosemarie, who had come along; "no finesse." Rosemarie spent the first part of the concert leaning against a wall. "I want to judge for myself," she said. She agreed with me when she returned. After the concert I asked Kraayvanger about his technique. "It is very difficult," he said. "There are thirty-five muscles to be considered." Weimar had excellent local singers—among them Rudolf Lustig, a native Viennese who later went to Berlin, Vienna, and Bayreuth; and Karl Paul, a powerful baritone but an indifferent actor. Hermann

Abendroth conducted the philharmonic orchestra. I heard Tchai-kovsky's Fifth—my favorite emotional mudbath at the time—saw *Don Pasquale* in Apolda with a vivacious Norina and Paul as Dr. Malatesta, and *Don Giovanni* in Erfurt with Karl Schmitt-Walter in the title part—a breathtaking performance. Rosemarie and I often read poems to each other—ballads, love poems, metaphysical stuff. Morgenstern's gallows songs were our favorites. Young poets sought me out and asked for my judgment; I have no idea why.

At the academy I took classes in Italian, harmony, piano, sing-ing, enunciation. Harmony, for some reason, involved singing scales and intervals. Not being able to read music, I pretended to be hoarse and finally stayed away altogether. Hauschild concen-trated on lieder, mostly pianissimo, mostly Schubert.

Maxim Vallentin supervised the acting and tried to reform the surrounding theaters. We, that is, Vallentin and assorted students from the academy, took a train to one of the many theaters of East Germany, bought tickets, and watched whatever was being of-fered. After the performance one of us—it might be a student, it might be Vallentin himself—would rise and ask the audience to criticize what they had seen. Most people stayed, out of curiosity, I believe, for this was a new experience. They stayed, but they didn't say anything. We had expected this and were prepared. Another student rose and made an intentionally confused remark. Then the next one would take over, this time with something clearer and more direct. Hearing ideas expressed in an unrestrained way, people who had never talked in public before became great ora-tors. Some even wanted their money back, especially in Erfurt, where we saw a hilarious *Faust.* I joined the Kulturbund zur Demokratischen Erneuerung Deutschlands (Cultural Association for the Democratic Reform of Germany)—the only *Verein* I ever belonged to—and participated in the meetings. I seem to have led a full life. Still, I was dissatisfied. As is my habit, I did not analyze the situation but decided to move.

Two days before my departure I went to a monster discussion about modern (i.e., antifascist) drama. Vallentin was there; so was Gerhard Eisler, brother of the composer Hanns Eisler, and high official in the East German government; there were playwrights, actors, producers, and students from the academy. After listening to about an hour of boring slogans and limping commentary, I got up and made a speech. I am not an accomplished debater, and large audiences scare me, but I was much too excited to remain silent. There are plenty of antifascist plays around now, I said; they are springing up like mushrooms after a summer rain. Unfortunately their quality is very poor. What is more, there is hardly any difference between them and earlier plays about the Nazi underground. In both cases we have Heroes, Villains, and Undecided Individuals. In both cases the Villain betrays the Hero—which leads to chases in the cops-and-robbers tradition. In both cases the Undecided Individual (usually a man) searches his soul and finally sees The Light, often with the help of an already enlightened Good Woman. There is a small difference—the leading arias mention Marx and Lenin here, Hitler there. But isn't it absurd to base the fight between good and evil on mere names, and isn't it rather obscene to use the same form, even the same type of story, to describe it? Many people seemed to agree, and Vallentin was intrigued, but there was no time to continue with the debate. Next day I attended rehearsals of *Tales of Hoffmann,* with Rudolf Lustig in the title role. The actors were partly in costume, partly in street clothes. I didn't know the plot, and couldn't distinguish between the play itself and accidents at the rehearsal; it was a strange experience, which stayed with me for years. The morning after, I left Weimar and started on my return to Vienna.

The first station was Munich. I went to the opera (*Freischütz,* with Ferdinand Frantz as Kaspar; and *Tosca,* with Georg Hann as a very crude Scarpia), bought food on the black market, had a look around, and took a fast train to Freilassing, the border town. There

I was stopped by the United States Army border police. They were on solid ground; my identification (a certificate of discharge from the hospital in Apolda) was a copy and looked suspiciously like a fake. I was locked up with a prostitute and a former general. After three days I was interviewed by a U.S. soldier and a Bavarian who spoke broken English—a slimy individual, eager to use the confusion for acquiring a position of importance. I was released, having been advised to return to Munich and to cross as part of a collective transport. A few days later I stood before our apartment house in Vienna: 15th district, Alliogasse 14. The housekeeper saw me first. "Jessasmariaundjosef!" ("Jesus Mary and Joseph!"), she exclaimed. Dragging myself along on two crutches ("totally unable to work," it says in my discharge papers) I was a sight indeed. I climbed up the three floors (we had no elevator), walked to the apartment, and rang the bell. My father opened the door. We embraced. I was home again.

6 University and Early Travels

My father had been alone since the death of mama. He had survived bomb attacks and had been for weeks without light, heat, or adequate food. To save money and material he slept on blankets instead of sheets and wore the upper parts of decaying shirts until they were too frayed to be seen in public. As a former member of the Nazi party he had to register with the authorities. He was afraid that he might be dismissed from his job and lose his pension.

I was vaguely aware of these problems but not really interested. Only much later did I realize how lonely my father must have been. Yet he never complained; he tried to help me as well as he could, with money, advice, moral support. He also ran the household. Once a week he threw all the edibles he could find into the big aluminum container mama had used to soak our dirty clothes, added water, salt, and spices, and made a soup. Every day we took a slice off the top and heated it. That was our only meal. We had no wood and no coal. The inside temperature during the winters of 1946 and 1947 was about 5 to 8 degrees Celsius. I spent most of the time in bed, reading and revising lecture notes; or I sat at the table, drank hot water, and covered myself with blankets. Yet I was not as bothered by events as I am today.

My academic dossier has two special entries. The first, dated November 18, 1946, says that I was checked by the faculty commission on ethics (*Ehrenkommission*) and admitted without preconditions. That was easy. I had not joined the party and I had not been involved in any criminal activities. I can't take credit for that—the occasion simply didn't arise. I don't know what I would have done had I been asked to become a *Parteigenosse* or ordered to kill civilians. The second item, dated January 28, 1949, reads: "In the course of restitution for war participants there is an exemption of two semesters: the dissertation can be handed in at the end of the sixth semester." I also got a monthly pension (I still have it). That puzzled me. We lost the war, I said to myself. How come I am getting all these privileges? At any rate, I was now a student. I was three to five years older than the rest and a cripple. It didn't seem to matter. I was treated as if I were eighteen and in perfect shape.

My original plan had been to study physics, mathematics, and astronomy and to continue with my singing. I chose history and sociology instead. Physics, I seemed to think (though my thoughts were not at all well articulated), has little to do with real life. History is different: history will make me understand what just happened. It did not. Pivec, who lectured on the history of the Middle Ages, started with statistics—the structure of the feudal system, the role of serfs, the size of individual possessions, and so on. I waited for juicy incidents; they never came. Lhotsky explained how the Hapsburg Empire had grown, by marriage and by accident, from small beginnings to its monstrous later dimensions. Santifaller, the chairman of the famous Institute for Austrian Historical Research (Institut für Österreichische Geschichtsforschung) and an expert in the analysis of documents, described the politics of the Austro-Hungarian monarchy during the late nineteenth century. I had the good fortune of hearing the art historians Demus and Svoboda. It was Svoboda who made me aware of Cimabue, Giotto, and the transition to pictorial realism. This interest lay dormant for over thirty years; then I read the literature, visited the major sites, and gave lectures on the subject. Today Giotto, with his determined stylization of events, is one of my favorite artists. So my excursion into history was not a total loss. At the time, however, I was dissatisfied and longed to return to science. I asked the dean for a transfer and finally attended my first physics lecture.

In 1947, Vienna had three well-known physicists: Hans Thirring, Karl Przibram, and Ehrenhaft. Thirring gave the standard lectures on theoretical physics—mechanics, thermodynamics, optics, the lot. He had calculated the relativistic consequences of the rotation of a material shell—the famous Thirring-Lense effect. He was an expert skier and an inventor with numerous patents to his credit. He had been fired in 1938 because of his "corroding" influence on the "military readiness of the nation," his opposition to fascism, and his friendship with Einstein and Freud. When he returned, he announced a course on the psychological and ethical foundations of world peace. "This is important," he said; "physics is not." Most of the students thought otherwise. They crowded into Thirring's physics classes—Thirring was an excellent teacher —but the Auditorium Maximum, where Thirring lectured on peace, was practically empty. Later, as a member of parliament, Thirring developed a plan for the disarmament of Austria. Austria would abolish its army and air force, and the surrounding countries would withdraw their units to a specified distance from the Austrian border; the arrangement would be guaranteed by the United Nations and the major postwar powers. It was a reasonable plan, but madness in the eyes of politicians and patriots for whom a country without planes, guns, or soldiers and without military noise for visiting dignitaries was a nonentity. Thirring occasionally came to the talks I gave while still a student. I visited him when on vacation from California, and I met him again during his trip through the United States. I admired him, but it is only now that I realize what a unique person he really was. Though he had strong commitments, he never lost his sense of humor. For him the tendencies he fought were proof of human folly, not of evil incarnate. He was that rare paradox—a skeptic committed to peace and humanity. What a difference from the grim-faced, guilt-ridden, teeth-gnashing, slogan-spouting apostles of humanitarianism who surround us today!

Przibram and Ehrenhaft ran the laboratories. Karl Przibram, a former pupil of J. J. Thomson (and editor of the well-known *Briefe zur Wellenmechanik*), was a quiet, elegant man who wrote tiny equations on the blackboard. He was easily flustered, especially when the noise from Ehrenhaft's class interfered with his teaching. This was Ehrenhaft's first semester back in Vienna. Strange stories preceded him. He had fought Millikan on the charge of the electron and had lost (the story of the battle is told by Holton in volume 9 of *Historical Studies in the Physical Sciences*). He had discovered magnetolysis (dissociation of water in a strong magnetic field) and magnetic monopoles of mesoscopic dimensions; he asserted that the inertial path was a helix, not a straight line; and so on. His views on theory were similar to those of Lenard and Stark, the leading proponents of a "German physics," whom he often mentioned with approval. Many scientists regarded him as a charlatan, and we, the physics and math students, intended to expose him.

Ehrenhaft exposed us instead. He performed his experiments, which were simple and rather straightforward, made a few sarcastic remarks about "those theoreticians," looked at us, and shouted, "Are you dumb? Are you stupid? Don't you have anything to say?" He used almost the same words when he addressed Rosenfeld, Pryce, and Walter Thirring (the son of Hans Thirring and also a theoretical physicist) after a lecture at the summer university in Alpbach. Many anecdotes circulated about his chutzpah; I'll mention three.

Ehrenhaft ordered expensive equipment from Phillips in Holland. After a few weeks, Phillips inquired: "Did you receive our equipment?" "Yes," Ehrenhaft replied; "and it is of excellent quality." The next letter was a little more direct; it demanded payment. Ehrenhaft was unfazed. "I, Ehrenhaft, certified that the equipment is of excellent quality. That is worth much more than the sum you mention in your invoice; in fact, I should be getting money from you." Second story: Ehrenhaft was dissatisfied with the situation at his institute. He went to the minister of science without having asked for an appointment. The secretary tried to stop him: "The minister is at a meeting," the secretary said. "What kind of meeting?" "A meeting with foreign educators." "That suits me fine," Ehrenhaft replied. He walked by the secretary and confronted the minister: "Do I get what I want or shall I tell these gentlemen how things are being run in Austria?" Ehrenhaft got what he wanted. The third story is true, and I am a witness. In 1949, Ehrenhaft came to the Alpbach summer school. He set up his experiments and invited everybody he could get hold of to have a look. The day before his lecture he pulled off a nice piece of advertising. Rising after a rather involved talk by Friedrich von Hayek, he said with wonder and respect in his voice: "Dear Professor von Hayek—that was a marvelous, a fine, a most learned lecture, and I respect you for it. I did not understand a single word." I can still see him before me, this mountain of a man, his eyes wide open, his hands extended in a helpless gesture, his face completely innocent. Next day he had an overflow audience.

Did Ehrenhaft convince anybody? He certainly did not convince the theoreticians (though Paul Dirac wanted information about the strength of his magnetic poles). The senior Thirring saw problems, but for the rest the phenomena Ehrenhaft produced in such abundance were simply a *Dreckeffekt*—a result of as yet unknown disturbances. An iron curtain formed by a firm belief in the excellence of Maxwell's equations, and so on and so forth, protected physics from Ehrenhaft—an iron curtain of precisely the kind that had protected Galileo's opponents. To penetrate the curtain we organized a special seminar, in which we tried to explain

Ehrenhaft's phenomena by orthodox theory. We didn't succeed. We were not converted either—we simply believed that a better and more sophisticated approach would do the trick. At the same time we remained staunch empiricists. Not a single one of us ever doubted that science had to be adapted to facts. Later on, this attitude—which I shared—made it clear to me that the day-to-day business of scientific research, or "normal science," as Kuhn was to call the process, could not exist without a split consciousness of this kind.

The following semester I took Ehrenhaft's lectures down in shorthand; I discussed the text with him and sold copies to the students. These are the only record of Ehrenhaft's ideas around 1947.

Twice a week I went to the observatory to attend seminars on radio astronomy, observational techniques, and perturbation theory. I soon discovered that the astronomers had no idea of theoretical cosmology, a subject I was interested in. To educate them, Erich Jantsch (who later became a self-organization guru) and I gave a series of special lectures (I used Heckmann's encyclopedia articles as a basic text). Kasimir Graff, the observatory director and an outstanding observational astronomer, shook his head in amazement as we piled formula upon formula without mentioning a single fact.

Downtown I listened to Radon (tensor analysis), Hlavka (algebra), Hofreiter (differential equations), Sexl (nuclear physics), Prey (spherical astronomy). Radon was an internationally recognized authority. He was also rather nervous. Once it took him two blackboards to derive $0 = 0$. "Das ist richtig," he said with sadness in his voice; "aber es hilft uns nicht weiter" ("It's correct, but it doesn't get us any farther"). Hlavka gave his lectures from notes written on the back of bus tickets—a rather impressive performance. Many women attended the lectures. Neither we nor the lecturers were surprised. Some of the weaker and lazier male students asked their female colleagues for assistance without feeling that their manhood had been damaged. All of us, men and women, were "scientists" and thus superior by far to students of history, sociology, literature, and similar trash.

After class—sometimes even between classes—I would take a look at the cultural life of the city. I attended discussions on politics, modern art, the existence of God, the theological implications of modern science. I took acting classes, resumed my singing lessons, and went to concerts, opera, drama. I saw Werner Krauss, that great magician of the theater, in Bruckner's *Elisabeth,* Hochwälder's *Öffentlicher Ankläger,* Hauptmann's *Vor Sonnenuntergang,* and as Wallenstein. I was disappointed by Krauss's *Hauptmann von Köpenick.* Here his acting seemed to have become routine. Curd Jürgens and O. W. Fischer were still at the Burgtheater. Jürgens was an impressive actor, but a failure as Kowalsky. I remember listening to Bruckner's Eighth Symphony. I had to stand throughout the performance—but although still on crutches I didn't even notice the two hours' walk home.

When Pabst returned, I played a small part in one of his films (Ernst Deutsch had the leading role). I defended modern artworks in letters to editors and in person, attacking critics who vented their anger at art exhibitions. Every Tuesday at seven in the morning I appeared at a theological seminar behind Saint Peter's to convince Father Otto Mauer of the futility of his efforts. Believing in God was one thing, I said. But trying to prove his existence was bound to end in failure—the idea of a divine Being simply had no scientific foundation. This, incidentally, was my line in all interventions: science is the basis of knowledge; science is empirical; nonempirical enterprises are either logic or nonsense. Along with a small group of science students I invaded philosophy lectures and seminars. We were impressed by Aloys Dempf, a thunderous orator and an outstanding scholar of medieval philosophy. For a while I could recite all the major Latin definitions of Aristotelian terms. Roretz seemed OK—here I discussed Kant's *Prolegomena*. I explained Carnap's version of semantics at a special sociology meeting with Knoll in the chair and Hans Weigel in the audience, and gave a thoroughly deterministic account of animal behavior in Kraft's seminar: Why does a bird start flying now rather than a little later? Because the surrounding air, light, etc. provide the needed initial conditions. I felt absolutely sure that no other account made sense. Remembering this attitude today gives me some insight into the power of metaphysical systems.

Many years later I learned about the background of the people I had attacked and began to appreciate their human qualities. Monsignor Mauer, for example, was a leading libertarian theologian; he represented an attitude that became explicit in Vatican II, and he valiantly, though unsuccessfully, fought the return of more dogmatic tendencies. He was interested in modern art and tried to incorporate it into the liturgy. He had a mischievous gleam in his eye and occasionally looked a little like the devil. He was quite a character. I could have learned a lot from him had I been a little less self-centered. I wish I could talk to him now—but he has been dead since 1973.

The impression that remains is that I "was everywhere where interesting things were going on, provoking people," as Alan Janik, an author researching Viennese affairs in the twentieth century, wrote in a February 1993 letter to me. Some philosophers preferred to remain undisturbed. Heintel, for example, simply threw me out. At any rate, I became known to various organizations and was approached by some of them.

It started with the Austrian College Society. The society had been founded in 1945 by Otto Molden, Fritz Molden (then married to the daughter of Alan Dulles, head of the Central Intelligence Agency), and other members of the Austrian resistance. In his book *Der Andere Zauberberg* (The Other Magic Mountain, Vienna 1981), Otto Molden describes the basic ideas and the events that led to the first summer school in Alpbach, a small village near Brixlegg in the Tyrol. Alpbach soon became a world center of intellectual, artistic, economic, and political exchange. A student having lunch might find himself sitting next to Lise Meitner, Bruno Kreisky, or Paul Dirac; he might run into Arthur Koestler, Anneliese Maier, or Ernst Krenek; or he might catch his girlfriend flirting with Etienne Decroux (that happened to me). I visited Alpbach about fifteen times, first as a student, then as a lecturer, and, finally, three times as the chairman of a seminar.

There were four types of events: seminars, plenary lectures, symposia, and performances (dances, plays, music recitals, and the like). Seminars were scheduled from nine to twelve in various rooms or in locations outside the village. Philosophers, for example, assembled under a large tree halfway up a hill, soon called the tree of knowledge. Plenary sessions with lectures and public discussion took place in the afternoon, artistic events (followed by parties, dancing, etc.) in the evening. People who later became famous appeared out of nowhere, stayed for a few days, and left again. One of them was Waldemar Kmentt, the future Kammersänger Kmentt. Helmut Qualtinger wandered around between the tables at which we assembled after dinner. Someone would invite him to sit down and would order some wine, and soon Qualtinger was giving a riotous performance. He became a truly great actor. Once in a while we organized a cabaret. Many affairs blossomed and wilted under the Alpbach moon.

In 1948, Maria Blach (later Maria von Pronay), the secretary of the Austrian College Society and a close friend, asked me to make records of the major discussions; in return, the society would pay for room and transportation. Being good at shorthand, I agreed. This was the most decisive step of my life. I would not be where I am today, with the pensions I am drawing, the ambiguous reputation I seem to possess, and the beautiful and kind woman who chose to become my wife, had I not accepted Maria's offer.

August 1948 was my first visit. I could hardly wait for the proceedings to begin. Impatiently I listened to the brass band and the introductory political speeches. Then came a little PR: twenty professors explained what they were going to do in their seminars. I was curious about Karl Popper, who ran the philosophy seminar. I had skimmed through his *Logik der Forschung* and had formed a mental image: he would be tall, thin, serious, slow and deliberate in his speaking. He was the very opposite. Walking up and down in front of the participants, he said, "If by a philosopher you mean one of those gentlemen who occupy chairs of philosophy in Germany, then I certainly am not a philosopher." The German professors—and there were many of them—were not amused. We students, however, found his speech rather refreshing.

During the first plenary session I almost fell off my chair; so much nonsense, so many errors! Didn't the learned gentlemen know anything? I made notes for the discussion, hoping to straighten them out. At last the lectures were over. I raised my hand. The chairman chose one Eminent Person, and the Eminent Person spoke. He chose another Eminent Person, and that Eminent Person too spoke at length without saying anything. Finally it was my turn. I got up and limped toward the front of the hall— that's where the comments had to be delivered. By the time I arrived I had forgotten everything. It didn't matter—excitement and a sense of mission drove me on. Ernesto Grassi and Thure von Üxküll had discussed truth in a way that struck me as empty rhapsodizing. I let them have it. I must have talked about ten minutes. When the discussion was over and I moved out into the sun, I suddenly had Popper at my side: "Let's take a walk," he said. We left the crowd and wandered along one of the many trails that led from the village toward the woods. Popper talked—about music, the dangers of Beethoven, the Wagnerian disaster; he criticized me for having mentioned Reichenbach's "interphenomena" (from his book on quantum mechanics), and he suggested we use

the familiar *du* form of address. In the evening he took me to a se-
lect meeting with Bertalanffy, Karl Rahner, von Hayek, and other
dignitaries: I, a mere student, and a beginner at that, had been
found worthy of participating in their sublime debates! I didn't
open my mouth. It was one thing to speak in front of two hundred
people—that was like a theatrical performance, intimidating, yes,
but manageable; it was quite a different thing to respond to personal remarks or to address a particular intent face. Besides, without a crowd there was not enough adrenalin to get me going.

Next I was approached by the communists. At that time Hans
Grümm, still a communist, turned up at almost as many meetings
as I did. He acted as a talent scout: promising individuals were introduced to leading communist intellectuals in the hope that they
would see the strength of the cause and join the party. Hans and I
had many things in common. We opposed religion and supported
science. But while I relied on the experience of the senses and on
logic (or what I thought was logic), Hans defended realism with
dialectics as his main weapon. He was older than I and a seasoned
debater. I was not impressed. I had heard realistic arguments before; as far as I was concerned they were all circular: you made an
assumption that contained a realistic core and then proved realism by revealing the core. It took Walter Hollitscher two years to
convince me that the circularity was practical, not vicious, and
that it was an asset, not a disadvantage. Walter started by pointing
out that scientific research was conducted in realistic terms. I
countered that scientists, unfortunately, had not yet shed their
metaphysical eggshells. Metaphysics or no, said Walter, scientists
achieve results that are accepted by everybody, including positivists, whereas if they had adopted an antiseptic language and
strict logic they would never have gotten anywhere. That shut me
up for a while—but a residue of doubt remained.

From physics, Walter moved to politics, which meant Marx
and Lenin. Here I resisted like a stubborn mule. Jacqueline, my

then wife, and I voted communist in one of the early Austrian elections, but that was all. I don't know why I resisted. I had no political convictions and knew far too little history and economics to give substance to my contrariness. Youthful elitism ("Marx is a propagandist, not a philosopher") and an almost instinctive aversion to group thinking may have played a role (it certainly did later when I encountered the Popperian Church).

Through Walter, I came to know Berthold Viertel, the director of the Burgtheater; Hanns Eisler, who accompanied me singing Schumann and some of his marching songs; and Bertolt Brecht. We met Brecht at a rehearsal of *Die Mutter* with Helene Weigel in the title role. It was a strange event. The actors were standing around while Brecht complained about the color of a barely visible pot. Brecht, Walter told me, was prepared to take me on as an assistant (in Berlin). I said no and stayed in Vienna. I once thought (and said so in print) that this was the biggest mistake of my life. Today I am not so sure. I would have liked to learn more about the theater, and from such an extraordinary man. I would also have liked to get some training in forms of communication different from the scientific essay. But I suspect I would have detested the collective pressure of the partly fearful, partly dedicated, and certainly pushy and closely knit group that surrounded Brecht.

When I first met Walter, I regarded him, as I regarded many others, as a source of doubtful ideas. Violetta, Walter's wife, watched with amusement as I changed from a debating machine into the semblance of a human being. Later, when living in California, I visited Walter whenever I went to Vienna. I didn't know much about his day-to-day politics. He seemed to follow the party line; but he got into trouble because he explained and defended "idealistic" subjects such as psychoanalysis and information theory. For committed liberals, Walter was beyond the pale: an intellectual who had become a slave of totalitarianism. For me,

Violetta and he were wonderful, gentle, humane friends. I was devastated when I heard that they had died, first Violetta and then, only a week later, Walter. Walter's last letter to me, written about a year before his death, was a reply to a letter of mine in which I had announced my fourth marriage and our intention to have children. "I did not think we could be politically active and have children," he wrote; "Now I am sure we were mistaken and we regret it."

During the academic year, the Austrian College Society organized lectures, symposia, and discussion groups. We, that is, the science students who had started disrupting seminars and the philosophy students who had joined us, wanted to establish a group of our own. I was supposed to be the student leader, Viktor Kraft the academic chairman.

Kraft had been a member of the Vienna Circle. Like Thirring, he was retired when Austria became part of Germany. He was an uninspiring lecturer but an astute and careful thinker. He had anticipated some ideas that later were associated with Popper. I made this clear when reviewing his *Allgemeine Erkenntnislehre* for the *British Journal for the Philosophy of Science.* Popper was not amused, though the original version of his *Logik der Forschung* contains the relevant acknowledgments. Kraft, however, thanked me for my "careful analysis." (I still have his letter.) Now Kraft, who knew most of us from his seminar, expressed the wish for a more permanent arrangement. This was the beginning of the Kraft Circle, a student version of the old Vienna Circle. We reserved a room at the Kolingasse, the headquarters of the Austrian College Society, and met twice a month. We discussed special scientific theories; for example, we had five meetings about non-Einsteinian interpretations of the Lorentz transformations. Our main topic was the problem of the existence of an external world.

As I see it today, we made two mistakes. We assumed that discussing an institution meant discussing its written products. More especially, we assumed that science was a system of statements. Today that seems a slightly ridiculous idea, and the Vienna Circle is blamed for it. But the emphasis on writing is much older. Judaism, Christianity, and Islam are all based on books, and nature, accordingly, was treated as a book written in a special and rather difficult language. We also assumed, at least initially, that a complicated issue involving major conceptual revisions could be resolved by a single clever argument. The idea is still around, though without its former influence. I read the early volumes of *Erkenntnis* and reported on them in a series of talks. I also made notes summarizing the arguments and my contributions to them.

After a few months of solitary quarrels we started inviting visitors. Hollitscher defended dialectical materialism, Juhos talked about the interpretation of mathematical statements, Elizabeth Anscombe tried to explain Wittgenstein, though without much success. This, we thought, was a particularly uninspiring kind of child psychology. Hearing of our reaction, Elizabeth suggested that I approach Ludwig Wittgenstein himself, who happened to be in Vienna. I went to the Wittgenstein family residence (not the house in the Kundmanngasse). The entrance hall was large and dark, with black statues in niches all over the place. "What do you want?" a disembodied voice asked. I explained that I had come to see Herr Wittgenstein and to invite him to our circle. There was a long silence. Then the voice—the housekeeper, who spoke from a small and almost invisible window high up in the lobby—returned: "Herr Wittgenstein has heard of you, but he cannot help you."

Elizabeth, who seemed to be familiar with Wittgenstein's peculiarities, suggested that I write a letter—"but don't make it too subservient." I wrote roughly as follows: "We are a group of students, we are discussing basic statements, and we are stuck; we hear you are in town—perhaps you can help us." Wittgenstein seemed to like what I had written. "I've received a rather nice letter," he said, again according to Elizabeth, emphasizing the "rather," and was thinking of coming. Now the science students balked. "Who is this guy?" they asked, "and why should we listen to him? Anscombe was bad enough!" I calmed them down and reserved a room. On the day of the meeting I had a cold. Being rather ignorant in medical matters I swallowed tons of sulfonamides and sat down in eager anticipation. The hour arrived. Kraft was there, the philosophers were there—but no Wittgenstein. Afterward, Elizabeth told me how difficult it had been for Wittgenstein to negotiate this particular event. Should he come at the correct time, sit down, and just listen? Should he come a little late and enter with a flourish? Should he come very late, simply walk in, and sit down as if nothing had happened? Should he come very late and make a joke? At any rate, I started summarizing what we had been doing and made some suggestions of my own. Wittgenstein was over an hour late. "His face looks like a dried apple," I thought, and continued talking. Wittgenstein sat down, listened for a few minutes, and then interrupted: "Halt, so geht das nicht!" ("Stop, that's not the way it is!"). He discussed in detail what one sees when looking through a microscope—these are the matters that count, he seemed to say, not abstract considerations about the relation of "basic statements" to "theories." I remember the precise way in which he pronounced the word *Mikroskopp*. There were interruptions, impudent questions. Wittgenstein was not disturbed. He obviously preferred our disrespectful attitude to the fawning admiration he encountered elsewhere.

Next day I was in bed with jaundice—the sulfonamides had done me in. But Wittgenstein, I heard, had enjoyed himself.

In 1949, '50, '51, and '52 I went on my first foreign trips—to Denmark (three times, I believe, including a summer university at Askov near Copenhagen), Sweden (Lund, Stockholm, and Uppsala), and Norway (a summer university at Ustaoset). The Austrian

College Society paid for the trip. In those years traveling was no fun. There were checks by the Occupation forces, and then again at the German and the Danish borders; the trains were slow, cold, and poorly equipped. It didn't bother me; transportation during the war had been much, much worse.

In Denmark I had a long conversation with Louis Hjelmslev, whose *Omkring Sprogteoriens Grundlaeggelse* I had just read. I met Tranekjaer-Rasmussen, who was continuing the phenomenological approach introduced by Edgar Rubin and had participated in some of his experiments. Jørgen Jørgensen, the author of a monster treatise on the history of logic and of a somewhat smaller book on biology, received me with great kindness and told me anecdotes about the history of theology in Denmark. In Sweden, Jacqueline and I first stayed at a hotel in Stockholm and then at students' quarters in Uppsala. I gave a talk on basic statements to the philosophical association, with Mark-Wogau (whom I criticized), Halldén, and Hedenius in the audience. Back in Stockholm I went to Wedberg's seminar on Berkeley and to Oskar Klein's lectures on the general theory of relativity. I understood Klein, but my Swedish was not good enough to keep up with the discussions at the seminar.

In Askov I also met Niels Bohr. He came for a public lecture and conducted a seminar, both in Danish. I had prepared myself by reading newspapers and philosophical articles, and I understood every word of the lecture. That was quite an achievement. Rumor had it that Bohr was incomprehensible in any language. At the end of the lecture he left, and the discussion proceeded without him. Some speakers attacked his qualitative arguments—there seemed to be lots of loopholes. The Bohrians did not clarify the arguments; they mentioned an alleged proof by von Neumann, and that settled the matter. Now I very much doubt that those who mentioned the proof, with the possible exception of one or two of them, could have explained it. I am also sure that their opponents had no idea of its details. Yet, like magic, the mere name "von Neumann" and the mere word "proof" silenced the objectors. I found this very strange but was relieved to remember that Bohr himself had never used such tricks.

In the seminar, I got lost once again. Bohr sat down, lit his pipe, and started talking. He forgot to draw, lit the pipe again, and so on until there was a mountain of matches right in front of him. He talked about the discovery that the square root of two cannot be an integer or a fraction. To him this seemed an important event, and he kept returning to it. As he saw it, the event led to an extension of the concept of a number that retained some properties of integers and fractions and changed others. Hankel, whom Bohr mentioned, had called the idea behind such an extension the principle of the permanence of rules of calculation. The transition from classical mechanics to quantum mechanics, said Bohr, was carried out in accordance with precisely this principle. That much I understood. The rest was beyond me.

When the seminar was over, I approached Bohr and asked for details. "You didn't understand?" Bohr exclaimed. "That's too bad. I never expressed myself so clearly before." Aage Petersen had warned me of the phrase. "Bohr always says that—but then he repeats his old explanations." Bohr repeated his old explanations all right, but with renewed vigor, for he had just heard of David Bohm's apostasy. "Can you understand that?" he asked with a puzzled look on his face. Unfortunately he was soon dragged away to another meeting. Years later I dreamt that I met Bohr again, that he recognized me and consulted me on important matters— he must have made quite an impression. On the other hand I also dreamt that I advised Stalin, but I never met *him*.

7   Sex, Song, and Electrodynamics

These were the years when I married, divorced, and became involved in a variety of romances. I met my first wife, Edeltrud, or Jacqueline as she liked to be called in Alpbach, in 1948. She came from the Slovenian section of Austria, studied ethnology, and spoke half a dozen languages. She was one of the secretaries to whom I dictated my shorthand notes. We married for practical reasons: in the 1940s only married couples could travel together or book a single room. I loved Edeltrud but was distracted by the many well-dressed and exquisitely painted ladies who added beauty and a taste of wickedness to the proceedings. Some of them seemed to be fascinated by me—by my reckless behavior, my big mouth, which they confused with intelligence, and my strange ways. Alpbach thrived on pseudo-intellectual encounters. Here was Kerenyi with an Austrian contessa, looking mysterious and far away ("he's running around while I do all the work," his wife complained to me); over there, Gemmell consorted with an admiring American student; Popper circled the village church with an attractive lady physician—he circled at eight, he circled at nine, he circled at ten. "What shall I do?" he asked me when his wife was about to appear. After Alpbach I visited my new acquaintances. We had tea, dinner; we went to the movies, to the theater, to clothing stores (some of the ladies wanted to transform me into something a little more elegant), and to more compromising places. I also made discoveries closer to home.

Inge owned the dairy store in the basement of the house where I lived. I had gone down there before to buy yogurt and other edibles. I started lingering when Inge took over—she was delightful company. We were soon going out together, to bars, to the opera, on extended trips. Inge had a motor scooter; I got on behind her, prayed to all the saints I could think of—and was borne away. Then her husband started following us. He jumped from behind bushes when we were strolling through a park, suddenly appeared when we were embracing on a bench, and followed us when we went out of town. "Gott im Himmel!" Inge exclaimed when she saw his car, and accelerated. On some occasions she almost lost me. Eventually the gentleman suggested a "man to man" talk. We met in a coffee shop. There we sat, Inge in the middle, the husband to her right, I to her left. I don't remember the details of the conversation, but it went roughly like this. He: "You can have her; I withdraw." I: "No, no, you are her husband—I withdraw." After that we all went home. An hour later, Inge phoned (which means she rang a downstairs neighbor, Frau Tiefenbacher, also a married woman who went out with papa), talked as if nothing had happened, and asked, "Well, where shall we eat tonight?" I hear that she got divorced and has remarried. Would I recognize her if I met her in the streets, now, over thirty-five years later? I am not at all sure.

One day I found a note in my mailbox—"My name is Sheila Porter. Elizabeth Anscombe sent me"—and a telephone number. I rang. "I don't want to disturb you. What would be a good time for a visit?" My reply (according to Sheila): "You'll always disturb me, so it really doesn't matter when you come." Soon after Sheila arrived, we got into an argument. According to Sheila, people could live together only when they had similar interests. For me, similarity of interests was deadly; it led to boredom and separation. Sheila came from South Africa; she had studied philosophy and was looking for a job. Perhaps through her brother (the music

critic Andrew Porter) she became the chief PR woman for the Co-
vent Garden Opera House and, after that, assistant to Sol Hurok.
When Hurok died, she moved to the City Opera, but she couldn't
get along with Beverly Sills. For some years she let me stay at her
place in London; in turn, she stayed for a year at my Vienna apartment. She also painted it—to my dismay. I recently got a letter
from her from New York, asking my whereabouts.

I have mentioned romances, conversations, excursions—but
not sex. The reason is not any reticence on my part. In many cases
the matter simply did not arise. We flirted and had a good time.

But sex was never far away. When it tried to move center stage
I usually took evasive action. After all, I was impotent and not
quite sure how the ladies would react to that predicament. More
than once I created puzzlement, even rage, when at a decisive
juncture I drifted toward the door and disappeared. When I did
end up in bed, either by accident or because my desires had gotten
the better of me, I paid careful attention to every movement I saw
and every sound I heard and tried to give satisfaction by means
different from the standard procedure (assuming there is a standard procedure). I seemed to succeed, at least on some occasions.
Not only that—some women told me they had never had such an
orgasm before. The trouble was that while I liked the initial stages
of an encounter and was more than happy to follow the cues and
explicit instructions I received, I never had an orgasm myself. Seeing the joyful contortions of my partners, I often felt rather absurd. A friend of Jacqueline's, a former member of the Yugoslav
Olympic team and an imposing woman, twelve years older than I,
tried to solve the problem, but without success. Still, we stayed together for two years—and now another difficulty arose: the more I
was in love, the more I hated the slavery it seemed to imply. Again
I took evasive action, this time of a different kind, but it didn't
work. The freedom I thought I had achieved was almost as suffocating as the obsession I wanted to leave behind. It took many

years before this cycle of dependence, isolation, and renewed dependence dissolved into a more balanced pattern.

About one year after my return from Weimar, I visited Vogel, my former singing teacher. He was now living in an attic and had to watch his expenses. He needed pupils who might bring him fame and fortune, not a limping invalid like myself—and he said so. He sent me to Anton Tausche, a well-known lieder singer and teacher. Thinking I was a bass, I started with "Auch ich war ein Jüngling"—that was all my voice was good for. "You are not a bass, you are a tenor," said Tausche, and changed the key. Again scales, Vaccai, Concone; after that the familiar Italian songs and arias: "Tre giorni son che Nina," "Caro mio ben," "Ombra mai fu." My voice blossomed forth. It was a world voice all right. Tausche pressed on: Verdi, Puccini, Bizet. He had me take part in a recital in the concert hall. My contributions: "Comfort ye" (being a show-off I never breathed through all the embroideries) and "Già nella notte densa" (in German) with a badly shaped but vocally excellent soprano. The critics compared me to Leo Slezak, who had sung heroic and lyrical parts as well as lieder. I thought I was better.

Readers who know only intellectual joys can hardly imagine the pleasure derived from using a well-trained voice that has power as well as beauty. Many singers have achieved a firm control of their voice; they can sing long and difficult passages without taking a breath; they can increase and diminish their voice in all ranges; in short, they are masters of their instrument. Yet their instrument lacks power, or it lacks beauty. On the other hand, there are singers with powerful voices who bellow their way through a song or an aria and are soon out of breath. When at my best, I could do almost anything with my voice. I could let it go, rein it in, produce the softest pianissimo, and could increase my volume without feeling that I was reaching a limit. Singing gave me a sense of great power. My voice also projected well; soft or loud, it could be heard anywhere in a large concert hall. And it was beautiful, at least while I treated it well. For me no intellectual achievement can give the joys of using an instrument of this kind.

To enlarge my repertoire I went to the opera (the Theater an der Wien; the big house had been destroyed by a bomb) as many as five times a week. I bought standing-room tickets, 25 cents apiece, went to the benches on the first floor and sat down in a place that, among standing-room regulars, had become "mine." This was the time when Kunz, Schöffler, Siepi, London, Weber, Alsen, Dermota, Patzak, Seefried, della Casa, conducted by Boehm, Krips, or Moralt, created what later became known as the "post–World War II Mozart style." George London had just arrived. He had lied his way into a job and was forced to sing, within a day, a part he didn't know, though he had said he did: Amonasro. He spent the night studying, and gave a riveting performance. We in the standing room, the only real experts in the audience (so we thought), loved his voice and were thrilled by his acting. After a few months he added Lindorf, Dappertuto, Coppelius, and Dr. Miracle (all of whom he made even more mysterious by singing the role in French), Boris (in Russian, the only part where his acting failed him), and Don Giovanni. To see him singing "Fin ch'an dal vino," almost motionless, slowly—very slowly—putting on a pair of white gloves, was quite an experience. London soon became a world star: Bayreuth, the Bolshoi Theater, the Met. Gradually his voice thickened and sounded forced. I noticed the change when he sang the Dutchman in Bayreuth—it must have been 1955 or 1956. Then I heard him as Scarpia, in a broadcast from the Met. It was painful. London retired early and went into administration. He traveled the world over to find young artists for an opera center in Los Angeles. He suffered a stroke, lingered for years unable to move, and finally died. I cannot understand why a life with so much promise should have come to such a miserable end.

Ljuba Welitsch sang Aïda, Donna Anna, Tosca, Tatjana, Salome. It is trivial to say that every voice has its own character and individuality. But Welitsch really stood apart. Bright, silvery, effortlessly rising above a huge orchestra, her voice sounded like an instrument become human. She did not make many recordings. There are excerpts from *Aïda, Tosca, Don Giovanni* (bad Italian sung at an incredible speed), *Eugen Onegin,* and *Salome,* and there are live recordings of *Salome* and *Don Giovanni* (with Gobbi, Kunz, Dermota, and Schwarzkopf, with Furtwängler conducting). Welitsch too was stopped by vocal problems and retired early. Being in need of money she played character parts (she was excellent and very moving as the foreign woman in Menotti's *Consul*) and appeared in movies and on television. In the 1960s she was a regular on *The Vikings,* an American TV show. A few days ago I saw her again, on German TV, seventy-five years old, with flaming red hair, a little dog on her lap also with flaming red hair, and as vivacious as ever. "Callas had all the luck," she said. "She got the rich men; mine were poor and they soon ran away." She came on like a naughty child, but one could sense the determination, the iron will, and the discipline that had turned her into a star.

I had seen Hotter as the Dutchman before the war and had been disappointed. There was nothing disappointing about his performance now. His voice seemed to have no limits—even at its strongest it sounded as if Hotter could easily produce twice or three times the volume—and possessed a unique quality. Hotter was an excellent actor, except in *Tales of Hoffmann,* where his interpretation (it was an "interpretation" all right) bordered on the ridiculous. I heard Paul Schöffler as Don Alfonso, Don Pizarro, Don Giovanni, the count in *Figaro,* Prince Igor. Hans Sachs seemed to have been written especially for him. While some singers wilt in the third act—even Hotter had his troubles—Schöffler gained in strength and seemed ready to start all over again. The *Otello* with Lorenz, Schöffler, and a variety of Desdemonas—Hilde Konetzni, Carla Martinis, and a very young Leonie Rysanek among them—

was one of the best I have ever seen. Lorenz moved through the part like a tornado—being felled by anger, rising again, and finally fading away in sorrow. The only singer who could be compared to him was Ramon Vinay.

I saw Furtwängler conducting *Fidelio* with Martha Mödl in the title role, and I went to almost every performance of *The Magic Flute*. One performance stands out: Julius Patzak sang Tamino; Esther Rethy, Pamina; and Kunz, Papageno. Patzak was often impatient. In *Tosca*, for example, he hurried the conductor along as if he wanted to get the whole damn thing over with. Now he seemed at ease. The scene before the temple, one of my favorite scenes in any opera, was perfect, especially when Schöffler appeared as the speaker. I have seen some very interesting productions since then, including Felsenstein's *Hoffmann*, *Don Giovanni*, and *Otello*, Chereau's *Ring*, Sellars's *Don Giovanni*, and a variety of Ponnelles. Only Ponnelle's *Serail* (with Harnoncourt conducting) compares with what I experienced as a student, on the benches of the first-floor standing section, in postwar Vienna.

In 1951 I finally received my doctorate. I had started calculating a problem of classical electrodynamics but seemed to be getting nowhere. But I did have my notes from the Kraft Circle. Although I had written them for my own interest, they contained arguments and were the right length, so why not turn them into an essay and offer that as a philosophy thesis? Thirring and Kraft agreed. They knew me well enough to pass me without a single question. Stetter, the experimental physicist, asked for experimental specifics that I didn't know, while I wandered off into theories that he didn't like. I survived. Kainz, the outside examiner, had requested three books: Nicolai Hartmann's *Ethics*, his own *Aesthetics*, and Falckenberg's *History of Philosophy*. The latter has long stretches of text interrupted by additional and more recondite information in small print. I learned the small print and used it in my answers. Kainz thought I had been especially thorough and spared me the rest. While this was going on, I discovered that Kainz loved to talk. So when the exam moved to his own book (which I had skimmed through but not really studied), I mentioned some doubtful points. I had done the right thing—Kainz kept talking almost continuously. "That was an excellent examination," he said when the secretary urged him on, and he gave me the top grade. Being now eligible, I applied for a British Council scholarship to study with Wittgenstein in Cambridge. I collected a few recommendations, passed the English test, and was accepted. Wittgenstein died, and I had to choose another supervisor. I chose Popper. In the fall of 1952, I left for England.

8   London and After

traveled with a suitcase but without a cent in my pocket. I had not needed money before—there was always somebody to pick me up. This time I got into trouble. The French porters who carried the luggage from the train to the Channel ferry almost lynched me, and the representatives of the British Council who expected us in London had an address, advice how to get there, but no funds for transportation. Bashi Sabra, who arrived with me (and who is now a professor at Harvard), lent me a few pounds. I took a taxi to the Mary Ward Settlement on Tavistock Place, my new home. I had a room with a bed, a gas heater, a table, a bookcase, and two chairs. The bath and the toilets were outside, the breakfast/dining room downstairs. The other occupants were secretaries, business people, aspiring actors, and students like myself.

Next day I had a look at the city. I visited the London School of Economics, obtained a seat at the library, bought books, and saw some movies. I had headaches wherever I went. It took me a few days to discover the cause—the omnipresent London draft. From then on I would sit in well-protected corners, away from doors and windows. At the settlement I built a tent. It covered the upper part of my bed and contained the table, a chair, and a typewriter. This was where I worked, slept, and received visitors. They had to crawl into the tent on their knees, bringing the second chair with them. The place was occasionally shown to outsiders: "This is how our guest from the continent is dealing with the draft."

After a week I went to see Popper. He was not as forthcoming as in Alpbach and called in a witness (J. O. Wisdom) for our first encounter. "What are your plans?" he asked. I had not expected the question, but I did have an answer. I had just finished reading Bohm's new introduction to quantum mechanics. It is not the usual kind of textbook; it does contain the standard calculations, but combined with detailed philosophical analyses: one chapter on physics, one chapter on philosophy (mainly Bohr). I suggested that I should write a review. Popper seemed doubtful, looked at Wisdom for assistance, got none, and dismissed me. After that I saw him twice a week, during his lecture and at his seminar.

The lecture started with a line that became widely known: "I am a Professor of Scientific Method—but I have a problem: there is no scientific method." "However," Popper continued, "there are some simple rules of thumb, and they are quite helpful." For example, assume we want to explain a thunderstorm by saying it was caused by Zeus. Is this a good explanation? It depends. Assume somebody asks how we know Zeus exists. The answer "Didn't you see the thunderstorm?" is unsatisfactory; it makes the explanation circular. Are there similar patterns today? Yes—ad hoc explanations. How can the circularity be removed? By making sure that what does the explaining is richer in content than the situation to be explained. The explaining principles should also have some kind of coherence, which is best achieved by introducing new entities such as forces, fields, particles, and so on. Having been introduced for the explicit purpose of explaining known phenomena, these entities were not known before, which means that we explain the known by the unknown, not the other way around as is often asserted. And so Popper went on, intentionally trivial or paradoxical, trying to show how simple ideas that were derived from equally simple requirements brought order into the complex world of research.

Then came attacks on "inductivism," the idea that theories can be derived from, or established on the basis of, facts. Those who emphasize empirical backing, said Popper, advise us to stay close to the facts, which means they try to be as ad hoc as possible. Ad hocness is out; hence the requirement of a close empirical fit must be replaced by the requirement to go as far beyond the evidence as possible. Metaphysics does go beyond the known facts and often contradicts them. Does this mean that science is metaphysics? It does not; scientific hypotheses can be refuted, metaphysical systems cannot.

All this was easier to understand and more plausible than the various forms of inductive logic I had found in Mill and Jørgensen. The argument which finally convinced me that induction was a sham and which Popper presented at a talk to the British Society for the Philosophy of Science (the argument is Duhem's—but Popper didn't say so) was that higher-level laws (such as Newton's law of gravitation) often conflict with lower-level laws (such as Kepler's laws) and therefore cannot be derived from them, no matter how many assumptions are added to the premises. Falsificationism now seemed a real option, and I fell for it. I occasionally felt a little uncomfortable, especially when talking to Walter Hollitscher; there seemed to be a worm somewhere in the woodwork. Still, I applied the procedure to a variety of topics and made it the centerpiece of my lectures when I started teaching.

Today I regard this episode as an excellent illustration of the dangers of abstract reasoning. There are lots of dangerous philosophies around. Why are they dangerous? Because they contain elements that paralyze our judgment. Rationalism, whether dogmatic or critical, is no exception. Even worse—the inner coherence of its products, the apparent reasonableness of its principles, the promise of a method that enables individuals to free themselves from prejudice, and the success of the sciences, which seem to be rationalism's main achievements, provide it with an almost superhuman authority. Popper not only used these elements, he added a paralyzing ingredient of his own—simplicity. So what's wrong with a coherent philosophy that explains its principles in a simple and straightforward way? That it may be out of touch with reality, which means, in the case of a philosophy of science, with scientific practice. A philosophy, after all, is not like a piece of music that can be enjoyed by itself. It is supposed to guide us through confusion and, perhaps, to provide a blueprint for change. Popper knew that a guide, or a map, may be simple, coherent, "rational," and yet may not be about anything. Like Kraft, Reichenbach, and Herschel before him, he therefore distinguished between the practice of science and standards of scientific excellence and asserted that epistemology dealt only with the latter: the world (of science, and of knowledge in general) must be adapted to the map, not the other way around. For a while I reasoned in the same way. It had been fun to heap scorn on venerable traditions by showing that they were "cognitively meaningless." It was even more exhilarating to criticize respectable scientific theories by raising the magic wand of falsifiability. I overlooked the fact that I made an important and by no means obvious assumption. I assumed that "rational" standards, when applied rigorously and without exceptions, can lead to a practice that is as mobile, rich, stimulating, and technologically effective as the sciences we already have, accept, and praise. But the assumption is false. Practiced with determination and without subterfuge, the doctrine of falsifiability would wipe out science as we know it.

There are a few episodes that seem to conform to the falsifiability pattern (my favorite example was the transition from the *horror-vacui* theory to Toricelli and Pascal—until I learned better). But the great majority of episodes, and especially those which, according to Popper, show science at its best, developed in an entirely different way. Therefore science is not "irrational"; every single step can be accounted for (and is now being accounted for by historians like Shapin, Schaffer, Galison, Pickering, Rudwick, Gould, Hacking, Buchwald, Latour, Biagioli, Pera, and others). These steps, however, taken together, rarely form an overarching pattern that agrees with universal principles, and the cases that do support such principles are no more fundamental than the rest.

At this point the arts and the sciences become rather similar. Byzantine art constructed faces in a severely schematic way, using three circles with the root of the nose as their center. The length of the nose equaled the height of the forehead and the lower part of the face—and so on, as described in the *Painter's Manual of Mount Athos*. The rules do give us faces—but in a single position (frontal), without details and without character. They conflict with almost everything outside a special Byzantine school of art. In the same way Popper's rules can produce a Byzantine science; they are not entirely without results. But these results are a far cry from the science of Newton, Faraday, Maxwell, Darwin, Einstein, and Bohr (Otto Neurath, long ago, criticized Popper in precisely this way).

In the seminar (which was held in the Graham Wallace Room, at the London School of Economics, right behind the restaurant) Popper announced that we, the students, would have to do the talking. Any subject was acceptable provided it had a point and was presented clearly. When I started teaching I adopted the same procedure, and I have been using it ever since—it certainly beats concentrating on a fixed topic with tons of literature handed out in advance.

After a few weeks, London was engulfed in the great and by now legendary smog of 1952. It was quite an experience. Outside you had to walk slowly—people were visible for only a few steps. Inside, the end of the dining hall seemed to disappear. At the Old

Vic I heard the actors' voices (Paul Rogers in *An Italian Straw Hat*), but hardly saw the actors. I was lucky to reach the theater at all. When I boarded the bus I asked the conductor to throw me out at the Old Vic. He thought I said "Aldwych," forgot to notify me, let me ride on until I was directly in front of the Old Vic, realized his mistake, and advised me to walk back over the bridge. On the way I met four members of the settlement. "Where are you going?" they asked. "The Old Vic." "That's where you're coming from," they replied, and took me along.

About that time, Elizabeth Anscombe, safely ensconced in Oxford, suggested that I visit her. That was another adventure. The morning started with a bang: the children invaded my bedroom and played war. "Peach," as Elizabeth calls her husband, moved around forlornly—until he had his daily fit of anger. Barbara, who was somewhere between six and eight, told me of her many lovers, invited me to have a look at her naked body, and offered lascivious kisses. "George Kreisel kissed me that way," she said. Jam, coins, pages of manuscripts could be found in the most unlikely places; amid all this was Elizabeth—distant, smoking like a chimney. Visitors dropped in, looked around, left again. I explained my views on scientific change to Geach, L. L. Hart, and von Wright. Major discoveries, I said, are not like the discovery of America, where the general nature of the discovered object is already known. Rather, they are like recognizing that one has been dreaming. Today there is a technical term for such changes—incommensurability. I didn't use the term and saw no need for a special word—the matter seemed obvious. Hart and von Wright thought otherwise. So did Popper when I repeated the story in his seminar.

For the remainder of my stay in London I concentrated on two topics: quantum theory (von Neumann and Bohm), and Wittgenstein. Von Neumann was not easy; I worked my way

through his book, page by page, and eventually wrote a critical review. Wittgenstein resisted in a different way. His writings sounded
like fragments of a novel, but it was not clear who the actors were
and what their actions meant. Anscombe had earlier given me
manuscript materials, including a photocopy of the "Remarks on
the Foundations of Mathematics." I found this manuscript ex-
traordinarily exciting but I could not say why. I had also read the
Investigations. Now that the work was published, I tried to get to
the bottom of things. I rewrote the text, turned it into a treatise,
and used four different symbols to signal my interventions: normal quotation marks for Wittgenstein's text, crosses for para-
phrases, stars for elaborations, and still another type (I have
forgotten which) for critical comments. I knew that Wittgenstein
did not want to present a theory (of knowledge, or language), and
I did not expressly formulate a theory myself. But my arrangement made the text speak like a theory and falsified Wittgenstein's
intentions. I gave the essay to Elizabeth for criticism. She prepared
an English version (my text was in German) and sent it to Ryle. He
sent it right back: "An efficient condensation, not a review." Malcolm was more yielding. And so the paper monster I had produced
for my own enlightenment was published in the *Philosophical Review* of 1955.

Today I would say that Wittgenstein severely reduced the independence of theoretical speculation. Having found a theory,
the proud inventor often thinks he or she has found a shortcut to
nature, society, human existence. A few words, a few formulas—
and the secret is revealed. But try to apply the words or the formulas to some concrete event such as the sorrow following the
loss of a friend, and the theoretician either will say that these are
subjective particulars, not "reality," or will use ad hoc hypotheses,
or will resort to so many shortcuts, approximations, and additional assumptions that we are no longer dealing with the theory

itself but with a complex system of more concrete ideas (Nancy Cartwright has interesting things to say about how this works in physics). I fully agree with such a debunking of pure theory. In a sense, I have become a Wittgensteinian (or a nominalist, to use a more traditional term).

As before, I did not live by thought alone. I resumed singing with an excellent teacher, and I inspected the theatrical scene. This was the year when Warfield and Leontyne Price sang *Porgy and Bess* at the Stoll, and when the Italian season, also at the Stoll, had Gobbi as Scarpia, Silveri as Iago, and de Santis as Otello. I saw Olivier as Archie Rice and Paul Rogers as Shylock. Like Ernst Deutsch in postwar Germany, Rogers showed a Noble Jew, pushed around by selfish and cruel individuals (a few years later Olivier omitted the first monologue and further trivialized the play). I felt that such an interpretation was as trite and misleading as the reverse interpretation Werner Krauss had offered in Nazi Germany.

"So at least we understand the poet's intention," writes Alexander Granach in his extraordinary autobiography:

> The play is a comedy, a merry game of love. The fun is in the fact that at first obstacles are put in the lovers' way—first they are threatened with great perils, first their life is made bitter and sour, in order that they may overcome the perils, the obstacles, by the sweat of their brows, so that, at the end, the song of love may sound even more sweetly, even more intimately, even more happily. Then everything becomes like a midsummer night's dream! Then everything is as you like it!
>
> Therefore, in this gay game, in this comedy of Venice, a black figure is needed, to frighten the lovers, to threaten them, so that the denouement in Act V, beginning with the poetic "The moon shines bright: in such a night as this . . ." may be resolved in the giving of the rings and a happy going to bed! Yes! Shylock was only a black obstacle, planned by the poet, a black fool, a wicked fellow, to be made a goat of at last.
>
> But, but, but . . . and here the world stops in wonder! If that was the plan, how does it happen that Shylock's defense becomes an accusation?

'If you prick us, do we not bleed? if you tickle us, do we not laugh? if you poison us, do we not die? and if you wrong us, shall we not re- venge?"

The answer must be a perfectly simple one. God and Shake- speare did not create beings of paper, they gave them flesh and blood! Even if the poet did not know Shylock and did not like him, the justice of his genius took the part of his black obstacle and, out of its prodigal and endless wealth, gave Shylock human greatness and spiritual strength and a great loneliness—things that turn Antonio's gay, singing, sponging, money-borrowing, girl-stealing, marriage-contriving circle into petty idlers and sneak thieves.

(*There Goes an Actor*, translated by Willard Trask, New York, 1945.)

Researching the role, Granach asked himself what Shylock might do after the trial. Would he be really finished, or would he be able to start a new life elsewhere? Might he not use his cunning to turn defeat into victory? Peter Zadek's Shylock (in his fourth production of the play) smells a rat and starts preparing for the future while the trial is still on. The attempt may fail—but a play performed with this possibility in mind towers above blandly hu- manitarian or anti-Semitic productions.

At first I would go out alone. I liked to be by myself—there was no need to pay attention to the mood of others, and I could rise and disappear whenever I felt so inclined. Gradually, however, some of the ladies at the settlement started looking rather attrac- tive. I wrote poems for one of them and accompanied another to her home near Peterborough. Papa was a minister with strong opinions; needless to say we were soon at each other's throats—in a friendly way, of course. I invited Hazel to Vienna, but having met Diana in the meantime I got a shock when she arrived; she cer- tainly had looked better in London. At school I met Watkins, who for some time was Popper's pit bull (and continued playing this role with me, in a more or less relaxed fashion, until Popper ex- communicated him); Sabra, whose lectures I attended when I returned to London in 1965; J. O. Wisdom; and Joske Agassi, who became a friend, in a manner of speaking.

Agassi had hesitated; he did not trust a former Nazi officer. Popper asked Joske to give it a try, and Joske did try. Sitting on a bus we were a formidable combination. I made a statement mezza voce. Joske countered, raising his voice a little; I replied, already in forte; Joske countered again, fortissimo—and so on until the other passengers told us to shut up. During our visits with Popper we chewed cookies and jumped from one topic to another. I remember attempting to explain von Neumann's so-called proof, without success.

Through Joske I met Margarete Buber-Neumann and Martin Buber. Margarete had been a political prisoner, first under Stalin and then, after the Stalin-Hitler pact, under Hitler. After the war she started lecturing about her experiences. Now she was attacked by academic leftists who resented her criticism of Stalinist Russia and accused her of being a CIA plant. Yet she was not bitter—only amazed at what people were capable of doing to each other. Martin Buber needed a translator for an acceptance speech (he had just received an honorary doctorate), and Joske suggested me. I met Buber in a hotel lobby near Hyde Park Corner. "Shall I translate for content or for atmosphere?" I asked, for the content was somewhat elusive. "Atmosphere!" said Buber. "Atmosphere!"

Joske was (and perhaps still is) a pushy fellow with high moral standards; he criticized me right and left. I argued with him on some occasions, gave in on others, but lacking an ironcast worldview I floundered about as I had done during the Nazi years. One example: in 1955 Arthur Pap asked me to translate his textbook on analytic philosophy into German. I began working on it. "You're a criminal," said Joske. "It's a bad book." Like a dummy I wrote to Arthur: "I am not going to continue with the translation—it is a bad book." Now the problem was not that I was following Joske despite a contrary opinion of my own; no, the problem was that my perception of things was unstable and could be changed very easily. I had thought that the book was all right; after Joske's criticism I no longer liked it. I think that many young people—say, between fifteen and seventeen or, today, between seven and ten—have similarly unstable perceptions and views. They see the world in a special way, and yet the slightest pressure can make them see it differently. A good teacher respects this instability. Unfortunately, most educators use it "to teach the truth," as they call the process of imparting their own puny ideas.

Joske urged me to become a faithful Popperian. I find this somewhat puzzling. As I have said, Popper's ideas were very seductive and I had fallen for them. So why did Joske try to push me further? My only explanation is that I had not fallen far enough and that my lack of commitment showed. Indeed, I always hesitated when it came to declarations of faith, in private, and even more so in public. Falsificationism, I seemed to say to myself, may be OK; but why should I act as if it were a sacrament? Why, for example, should I put Popper on every page and into every footnote of everything I wrote? I was not reluctant to explain how much I had learned from Viktor Kraft, who had read my thesis and suggested improvements, or from Thirring, who was not only an intellectual but also a moral example, or from Hollitscher. That was a personal matter; I was grateful and said so. Here, however, I seemed to be entering the domain of religious PR, group dynamics, or intellectual greed—none of which was my cup of tea.

Early in 1953, Popper applied for an extension of my scholarship. He failed. "It doesn't matter," he said. "I'll ask for extra funds and you will soon be working as my assistant." I left London in the summer of 1953 and returned to Vienna.

Here I became involved in a variety of projects. Popper asked me to translate his *Open Society*, Kraft suggested that I write articles (on methodology and the philosophy of nature) for a French encyclopedia, and the Library of Congress wanted a survey of postwar academic life in Austria. I accepted all offers—I had nothing to do and I needed the money. Translating Popper was easy. I typed the first draft on an antediluvian typewriter, revised it a few times, and dictated the final version to a secretary. Still unfamiliar with the intricacies of the English language and preferring paraphrase to translation, I drifted away from the original, and Popper was not too happy with the result.

I read almost all the relevant literature for the encyclopedia articles and wrote an excellent text with detailed bibliographical essays. The editors made sizable cuts and omitted the bibliography altogether. The Austrian survey involved some library work; in addition I visited university institutes and private organizations, and I talked to professors, assistants, politicians, psychoanalysts, journalists, etc., etc. Viktor E. Frankl invited me to listen to a lecture he had given the day before; he put the tape into the recorder, started the machine, and sat down in an attitude of joyous anticipation. The machine said, "Ladies and gentlemen, today we have . . . ," and then fell silent. The microphone had become disconnected and Frankl had spoken to a mere fifty people, not to posterity. The final product was fairly complete (two hundred single-spaced typewritten pages, in a condensed style) and gave a good impression of what had been achieved since 1945; but again it was not published as I had written it: the translator (the essay was in German) omitted about one-third of the text and mutilated the rest. I received 1,000 shillings for my pains—not to be sneezed at.

I also had my first professional opportunity as a singer, and loused it up. Schachermeyer, who had heard me at one of Tausche's soirées, wanted to produce *Manuel Venegas* with me in the title role. I borrowed the score, went to the piano my neighbors had stored in my flat, and hammered out my part (I still could not read music). I knew three pages when I arrived at the rehearsal.

Schachermeyer sat down and played the introduction. Very flow-ery, lots of notes I had never heard before. I got confused, excused myself, and ran away. I should have hired a vocal coach; being a quick study, I would have learned the stuff in no time and could have given a rousing performance. I just didn't think.

At about that time Popper wrote that my assistantship had been approved. It was an honor and, besides, meant an end to my financial troubles; yet I felt quite uncomfortable. I couldn't put my finger on it; I only knew that I wanted to remain in Vienna. After some hesitation I declined the offer. Years later I found out how lucky I had been. Joske Agassi, who took the job, had very little privacy.

I was lucky even in the short run. On one of my visits to the philosophy library I noticed a young man I had not seen before. "I am Arthur Pap," he said. Arthur Pap—I knew him! I had read some of his papers in the journal room of the American Information Center and had found them interesting, and I told him so. He in turn was looking for an assistant. We quickly agreed on the terms, and I was in the money for at least another year.

When I met Arthur he was well established, which means he was known and appreciated by analytic philosophers, maligned by their opponents, and disregarded by administrators. He had a knack for identifying the simple assumptions behind an imposing formal argument, and he proved it in a seminar on Russell's *Princi-pia*. He also lectured on analytic philosophy. I took the lectures down in shorthand, typed them on stencils, and made copies for the class, for Pap, and for the publishers. The book—*Analytische Erkenntnislehre*—appeared in 1954.

Arthur had enormous talents. He had studied music and still excelled at the piano. After switching to philosophy he worked with Cassirer and wrote a splendid essay on the a priori in physical theory. He then joined the analytic movement, made important contributions, and published a textbook. Gradually he read less and wrote more; his writing became thin and unsubstantial. He could be rude, almost cruel. "If you were not a Jew you would be a Nazi," his wife Pauline exclaimed during an argument. Yet I had great affection for him and was saddened when I heard of his early death. Once I succeeded in dragging Arthur away from his papers; leading him to my piano, I opened a Schubert album, and we started a little concert—one song after another. He became a different person; he smiled, was almost happy. But the smile waned; he became restless, mentioned his work, and returned home.

So I was quite busy—but I was at a loss what to do in the long run. I felt I should make a move but had no idea what kind of move it would be. I played in a few more concerts, prepared for a job (which I never took) at a radio station, reenlisted at the university, and visited some society ladies while their husbands were away. I also wrote papers for assorted journals, one of them rather good. Then I received a letter from Anscombe: there is a job at Oxford, it said; why don't you apply? Why not indeed, I thought, and applied for all the available jobs I could find—one in Australia, one at Oxford, one at Bristol. I asked Popper and Schrödinger for recommendations. Popper had a problem; he had already promised his support to someone else for the Bristol position, but he helped me anyway. Early in 1955 I was invited to Bristol for an interview. Thus began what is technically known as my career.

9 Bristol

Having arrived at the University of Bristol I visited Koerner, the head of the philosophy department and chairman of the interview panel. He described the arrangements and introduced me to the committee: the president of the university, a short and lively man with a great sense of humor; Maurice Pryce, a theoretical physicist; Lang, a solid state physicist; and other assorted characters. I had never met any of them and knew nothing of their habits or achievements. On page 278 of his 1985 book *Bird of Passage,* Rudolf Peierls says of Pryce, "He could be a devastating critic and it is said that after each of his visits to Harwell someone had to go round to comfort the young people he had seen and assure them there was still a chance they might turn out to be competent theoreticians." I can testify to Pryce's destructive propensities —I was soon going to experience them myself. On the other hand, I helped him, somewhat to his surprise, when he got stuck in a lecture on quantum mechanics. But all that was still in the future. What I then saw was a row of faces, some expectant, some bored, some impatient—about fifteen of them—and I was ready for battle. Koerner asked about my studies, my interests, the things I had read. At one point (so Koerner told me) Pryce objected, "But this is not a philosophical problem." "It's a problem," I am supposed to have replied; "and that's good enough for me." I got into hot water when I said that my favorite theory of planetary origin was von Weizsäcker's. "Can you give us a brief account of it?" asked Pryce. I

could not, for I had never read it. There was an awkward pause—
and then the committee pressed on. When they had finished, I
gave a little speech. I don't know why; but it was a hot day, I was
excited, and I just could not stop talking. "You are scientists," I
said. "That doesn't mean you know everything. As a matter of
fact, you often make mistakes, especially in areas such as philosophy which you regard with contempt and yet constantly use,
though in an uninformed manner. But the mistakes can be
avoided since there are people who can help you"—meaning myself. I left the same day and went back to Vienna.

I was turned down in Australia and at Oxford—but I got the
Bristol job. Only much later did I realize how lucky I had been.
Bristol was the leading redbrick university in Britain, with an excellent reputation in the sciences; Mott had been there; Pryce and
Cecil Powell (discoverer of the pi-meson) were still teaching;
Shepherdson worked in mathematics, Koerner and Carrè in philosophy; L. C. Knight, the great Shakespearean critic, taught literature; Kitto was there—and so on. I was a newcomer, unknown to
the establishment, without publications or previous jobs to give
me substance, and a foreigner at that. I guess Popper was of some
help. The scientists, I heard, were impressed by Schrödinger's recommendation and by my big mouth. Now my future was safe for
at least three years—an eternity at that age.

During the summer I went back to Alpbach. This time I met
Philipp Frank, Alf Ross, Bergsträsser, Redlich, Giulio Carlo Argan,
Mitscherlich; we had song recitals by Christa Ludwig, who came
from her triumph as Cherubino in Vienna, and by Julius Patzak,
who sang Krenek's "Reisebuch," with Krenek at the piano. Bergsträsser almost strangled me when I made fun of his public speech,
and Mitscherlich was not too happy when I declared the soul to be
a social chimera. Alf Ross criticized the speed of my interventions
and tried to slow me down, occasionally by unfair means. I also
appeared in a cabaret. I changed clothes, put on makeup, sang a

ballad, and acted in brief sketches. Thunderous applause greeted me when I returned to the dining hall as myself.

Philipp Frank was a delight. He was widely informed, intelligent, witty, an excellent raconteur. Given the choice of explaining a difficult point by means of a story or of an analytical argument, he would invariably choose the story. Some philosophers didn't like that. They overlooked the fact that science, too, is a story, not a logic problem. Frank argued that the Aristotelian objections against Copernicus agreed with empiricism, while Galileo's law of inertia did not. As in other cases, this remark lay dormant in my mind for years; then it started festering. The Galileo chapters of *Against Method* are a late result. I met Frank again in Cambridge, on my way to Berkeley and a few years before his death. I had heard that he had fallen ill, and Joske and I went to visit him. We were shocked. Frank was completely senile— probably a victim of Alzheimer's, in today's diagnosis. There were moments of clarity—"It will soon be over," he said; "don't worry"—but they didn't last.

After Alpbach I returned briefly to Vienna. Sheila Porter was still living in my apartment, but we hardly saw each other. Late in September I packed my belongings and left for Bristol.

My job was fairly simple: I had to give a course on the philosophy of science for ten weeks, one hour a week. I had never studied the subject. I had read some books, but I suspected they would not get me very far. To find out how far, I wrote everything I could remember on a piece of paper. It barely filled a page. Joske calmed me down: "The first line here," he said; "that's your first lecture. You state what you are going to say; after that you elaborate— you'll remember lots of things once you get going—then you repeat and summarize, and before you know it, the hour will be over. Then comes the second line—and so on." I followed his advice, composed my first lecture, and learned it, in front of a mirror, like a part in a play—how else does an actor prepare himself for a new part? Things went all right from my point of view; I didn't get stuck, and term was over before I ran out of material. There were about twelve students, in a small room next to Koerner's office.

It was not easy to find a place to live. I had arrived late, and most of the better apartments were already gone. I got a couple of dark rooms with a hall, a kitchen, and a bathroom on the ground floor of a house behind the university. The hall had a glass roof, which meant that activities there and in the bedroom could be watched by the upstairs neighbors. One of them was a friend of the departmental secretary. It took me a long time to figure out why after an adventurous night she always received me with a knowing smile.

My time was now divided between reading, the radio, lectures, the staff seminar, a few dates, office hours, and the theater. The green Penguin mysteries were a real find. I devoured five or six of them per week and soon exhausted the stock of the local bookstore. I was fascinated by Hilda Lawrence. Rereading her work about thirty years later, I found her plots interesting but far less mysterious than in 1955. Is that what one calls a growing sense of reality? Slowly I branched out into other genres. One day I read a story in which events accumulated at an astounding pace, without much rhyme or reason, except for a girl called Rosa who, dead in a sack, turned up in unlikely places. She held the plot together. "Who is this guy?" I exclaimed, and looked at the title page. "By Damon Runyon," it said. Damon Runyon. I was hooked for life.

Having a salary at last, and a huge one from my point of view (£90 a month!), I could afford a little luxury. I got myself a telephone—my first telephone anywhere. I went to every new production at the Bristol Old Vic, which at that time was the best theater outside London. Peter O'Toole played Hamlet and Estragon; he appeared in *The Rivals,* in *Lear,* and in other plays. He took his acting lightly and occasionally started giggling for no reason whatsoever. Alan Dobie was excellent in humorous and nasty parts, and Rachel Roberts, soon to be one of Rex Harrison's wives, gave a wonderful performance in Ugo Betti's *The Queen and the Rebels*. I saw Tennessee Williams's *Camino Real* and became an instant admirer. In London, *Otello* was announced with Vinay and Gobbi. Gobbi didn't come; he was replaced by Otokar Kraus. That left Vinay. His once mighty voice had shrunk to a small volume, but his acting was extraordinary, microscopically detailed and yet without loss of grandeur. Years later I saw Vinay again, in San Francisco, as Falstaff. His voice had improved; it was not large but it projected well, and one could understand every single word. I don't know of any other case where a baritone (as Vinay had started out) turned tenor and then again became a baritone. I also found a lady or two to take to tea, dinner, and/or bed. Still, there were many lacunae.

I was interested in intellectual problems, took part in discussions, wrote papers, and gave talks. But when the papers were written, the talks delivered, and the discussions disposed of, I didn't know what to do. I had prepared myself for the theater and knew a few parts, and I believed that ideas were best introduced on a stage. Nothing ever came of it. I was often in love, and passionately so, but my emotions changed when the affair which, to me, was mostly a matter of the imagination seemed to become real. Almost all my actions were tentative, unfinished, without an overall purpose. Perhaps I liked too many things and was reluctant to be nailed down. There were long stretches of loneliness and boredom when I wandered around, during the day or at night, hoping that somebody, preferably a woman, would appear and set things right. Later, in California, my restlessness became intercontinental—I had one job, took another and still another, until I spent most of the time in the air. I flourished when confronted with an outside challenge; I shriveled when thrown back on my own resources. For about a year I took Seconal every day and slept night and day except for lectures and singing lessons. I was truly "killing time." In a way I was waiting for my life to begin—tomorrow, I thought, or next week, or next year everything would fall into place. Yet, in the midst of this emptiness I wrote papers and sketches that didn't merely make technical points but showed a simple and unreflected concern for others. How could that be? Where did the concern come from? I was often in pain—a result of the injury I had received during the war. The pain crept up on me, established a bridgehead, expanded, and stayed for hours, even days. I took painkillers, first the regular dose, then twice the dose, then up to five times the dose; I was sick—but the pain remained. Slowly, very slowly, the situation changed. My activities, interests, the things I wrote, said, attended to began to merge. It was like becoming a person with a character, an attitude, a point of view, and relatively stable aims. Singing, my ancient dream, was out of the question. So was writing plays, the next best thing as far as I was concerned. What remained was the possibility of arranging ideas and impressions like colors or shapes while preserving their dramatic potential. I also received outside help—quite undeservingly, I would say, but I did get it. But all this is as yet in the distant future. It is now 1955. I have just become acquainted with my second wife, I am supposed to give a lecture course on quantum mechanics, and I have been invited to chair a seminar in Alpbach, with Alfred Landé as my co-chairman.

Mary O'Neill was a student in my class. She had missed the first sessions, for she had been ill. Roy Edgley described her with enthusiasm and I became curious. I don't know how it all started: Did I invite her? Did we simply drift together? At any rate, we were soon going out at least once a week and having a good time. In 1956 Mary accompanied me to Alpbach (with her brother as chaperone). On our return I was inspected by the family—mama, papa, uncles, aunts. Part of the family came from Ireland, part from Wales. Some relatives had their doubts about this foreigner who walked around with a crutch and talked with a heavy accent. Mary herself seemed to hesitate—but a masterful performance on my part, full of passion and despair, finally brought her around.

The wedding was a big show—choir, organ, incense, the lot. I used my last £10 to buy a suit and looked rather impressive. We went to London for our honeymoon and afterward settled in an apartment in Bristol owned by Mary's parents. Then things slowly started falling apart. I think it was I who suggested that Mary move to the second bedroom. Soon I practically lived in my study or my office writing "important papers." "You are a cruel person," said Carmen, a Spanish instructor in Bristol who knew a little about our lives. I tried to change, but it was too late. At Christmas 1957 Mary visited her parents without me; she also had an affair. The last time I saw her was in 1958, at the railway station in Bristol. It was an accident; I was only a few steps away but I kept quiet. She is now about sixty. I know she has children, and I try to imagine what she looks like. A little rounder, some gray hairs perhaps? Thinking back, I am appalled at the waste—the waste of the affection and love that was there in the beginning but turned into sorrow, fear, and hatred because of my actions.

The course on quantum mechanics was a disaster. I had read technical books and papers, I had memorized what I thought were important calculations, but I was too close to particulars to see their overall import. Pryce did not make life easier. "Meaningless words ungrammatically used!" he exclaimed after one of my explanations. I started with about eighty auditors from all faculties—the topic was as fascinating then as it is today; in the end I was left with ten bedraggled faces.

The Alpbach seminar went much better. I knew Landé's latest book and had written a review. The book has a formal part, which is not difficult to understand, and a philosophical part, in which the formal steps receive an interpretation. I treated rival inter-

pretations in a similar way, that is, I separated the formalism from
the accepted reading and examined various versions of the more
prominent steps. The seminar grew larger than we had planned.
The historians de Santillana and Schimank were without students
and joined us; so did Schrödinger. He was not too fond of Landé's
approach, spoke highly of Ernst Mach ("wir können doch nicht
hinter Mach zurückgehen!"—"We can't go back behind Mach!"),
frequently mentioned the second quantization, which he regarded as a possible way out of trouble, and objected strongly
when de Santillana produced a diagram showing that Copernicus
had as many circles as Ptolemy. Wolfgang Pfaundler went around
taking pictures. I have one of them. There I am with my mouth
wide open, a startled Heinz Post opposite and an embarrassed
Landé to my left.

The third quantum event I became involved in was the Colston Research Symposium of 1957. Still being impressed by formal
tricks, I prepared a lecture on the quantum theory of measurement. I also participated in the discussions and edited the proceedings. My lecture was not particularly original. Still, it did clear
up a few points of von Neumann's theory, and van der Waerden
has praised it as recently as 1985. Michael Scriven, who attended
the symposium as a representative of the Minnesota Center for
the Philosophy of Science, invited me for a visit. I went to Minnesota during the summer and talked about the role of the ergodic
principle in statistical thermodynamics. There I met Feigl, Hem-
pel, Ernest Nagel, Sellars, Hilary Putnam, Adolf Grünbaum, Maxwell, Rozeboom, and others.

Later that year, I took a closer look at the British philosophy
establishment. I already knew John Watkins. He was not exactly
establishment; he was a Popperian but well settled in this particular role. Dinners with John were carefully choreographed. He
would welcome me at the door, take me up to his study, and invite

me to take a seat. Walking up and down with a stern face he would chastise me for having been a bad Popperian: too little Popper in the text of my papers, no Popper in the footnotes. Having explained in detail where and in what manner Popper should have made an appearance, he would heave a sigh of relief, lead me to the dining room, and allow me to eat. Imre Lakatos, whom I met much later, attacked me in almost identical terms: "Why did you say X when Popper says Y, and why don't you mention Popper who, after all, also said X on a few occasions?" I hear that even now the sacred word POPPER continues to give strength to the faithful.

I attended meetings of the Aristotelian Society and saw some rising stars in action. I was amazed at their lack of dialectical finesse. Once, at dinner, I sat next to Ryle. I had admired his *Concept of Mind*. Now I loved his dry wit and his sense of perspective. "Clever and mischievous like a barrel of monkeys," Ryle is supposed to have said about me. In 1958 I gave two presentations myself, one in March, in London, with Ayer in the chair, the other in summer, in Southampton, with McKay as the second contributor. During the academic term I visited various redbrick universities. In Birmingham I gave one of my standard talks about quantum mechanics. In the course of the discussion an elderly gentleman asked some questions and raised an objection. Assuming that he was unfamiliar with the theory, I explained it in simple and elementary terms. The gentleman listened patiently, nodded his head, and thanked me. Next day I heard I had been instructing Rudolf Peierls, a well-known physicist, nominated for a Nobel prize.

In 1958, three years after I had started in Bristol, I was invited to spend one year at the University of California in Berkeley. The invitation came at the right time. Mary had left. There was little else to keep me in Bristol. I accepted, packed my belongings, took a train to Southampton and a boat to New York. From there I went to Pittsburgh to visit Adolf Grünbaum and then to Princeton for a conference. I arrived in the early afternoon. Wandering around, I found a movie theater and saw *The Fly*—a fitting introduction to my long American adventure.

10   Berkeley—the First Twenty Years

spent forty years in English-speaking countries, thirty-two of them in the United States. Austrian culture—whatever that might be—had hardly affected me. My parents came from rural areas, my father from the German-Slovenian part of Carynthia. I was born in Vienna, grew up in Vienna, and went to Viennese schools. But when I was small my parents kept me off the streets, and when I was larger I stayed off the streets myself. Apart from choral practice, visits to the opera, or attending astronomy courses, I remained home and read books—adventure stories, love stories, mysteries, plays, and, later, books on science and philosophy. The novels and plays either were by German writers (Goethe, Karl May) or were translations into German. I was interested in action, not in style or character. One might say that I absorbed a small section of world literature—nothing specifically Austrian. I disliked the Viennese dialect and spoke either a neutral German or a stage German with a Prussian accent. Reading cultural journals of the Nazi period such as *Das Reich* gave me a glimpse of the "German mind," but the impression didn't last. Besides, I never read the works or looked at the pictures that were being discussed. My stint in the army—three years, 1942–45—was an interruption, a nuisance; I forgot about it the moment it was over. Soon I couldn't even imagine having been first a common soldier, then a lieutenant, then the commander of an entire battalion, running up and down the Russian countryside. Was it a dream? Was it reality? How did I manage to survive? True, I had a reminder: I was and I still am limping around with a cane. But I grew accustomed even to this predicament. Today I wonder how people manage to stand or walk without any extra support. Today their state, not mine, seems to be in need of explanation.

When I arrived in England, I realized of course that I was in a foreign country; the language was different, and so was the money. But the people seemed to be more or less the same, and the books I read—the novels, the plays, the physics and philosophy books—opened no new cultural perspectives; they simply added to what I had already absorbed. America was the first country that gave me a vague idea of what a culture might be. By American culture I don't mean Thoreau, Dewey, James, Stevens, or Henry Miller but Hollywood, vaudeville, musicals, wrestling, soap operas, stand-up comedy, Spillane, Chandler, Hammett—in short, show business and pulp. (Later on I added cultural and racial diversity; one of the reasons I did not want to return to Europe was the monochromaticity of its population.) I regret having left all that behind—the language, the humor, the casual way of approaching a topic, the strange world that sustained a Mack Sennett, a Joe McCarthy, a Busby Berkeley, and a George Bush. And yet I often wanted to get away. Slowly I shall forget—first the feelings, then the images, then even the words, and a large part of me will vanish without a trace.

A few weeks ago I found some notebooks covering part of the period between 1960 and 1972. Like many other documents they survived by sheer accident. There are comments on plays, movies, concerts, and operas, long excerpts from books, and descriptions of people I had met. Detailed reviews of performances and books alternate with stream-of-consciousness accounts of my moods; comments such as "I have to leave Berkeley"; "I can't stay here any longer"; "this is a cultural desert—I am suffocating" occur on almost every page, especially after visits to London. Very, very slowly I adapted to the Californian way of life. Indeed, I might still be in California and might have been buried, burned, or eaten there had I not been chased away by the October 1989 earthquake.

I arrived in September 1958. Ernie Adams, a future colleague, collected me from the airport. We drove to his place, had dinner, and I stayed overnight. We quarreled about Beckett's *Waiting for Godot;* he praised it, I thought it was the pits. Next day I got a smelly room in a flophouse on Telegraph Avenue. Being concerned more with practicality than with elegance, I might have stayed for years, but Margot objected. "Either you get another place or you won't see me again." I started looking around. I found a small apartment atop a set-back garage on Hillegass. The situation was perfect. I had a home all to myself and was protected from the street noise that had disturbed me at the hotel. The rent—eighty dollars a month; hard to believe today. I moved again when the landlady took over. After a brief stay on Benvenue, I rented a huge wooden box at 6041A Harwood Avenue in Oakland. It had a loft for the bed, a large working area downstairs, enormous picture windows, and a backyard. In the winter of 1969/70 I bought my first house in the Berkeley hills. I lived in the basement while some renters, left over from the previous owner, occupied the upstairs. After a few weeks I discovered I had company—a rat that lived right under my bed. Remembering that Lenin had called Kautsky (the Austrian socialist) a rat, Robin called my rat Kautsky. Kautsky got on my nerves, and I started distributing poison. The rat disappeared and was replaced by a penetrating stench. I called one rat expert. He was a young man with impressive equipment—a rat engineer, no less. He looked around. "We may have to tear the walls down," he said. I called another expert. He had no equipment at all except that he looked very much like a rat. "Rats deceive you," he said. "The stench is in one place, but the rat is in another." He disappeared and in a few minutes returned with Kautsky, or what was left of him. I soon left myself—the house was on a main road and was too noisy. I still own the house I bought afterward, 1168 Miller Avenue, but I hope to sell it for a good price in the not too distant future.

Margot, who had started this development, was the daughter of one of my colleagues. We met at a departmental party, went to movies, to the theater, and to bed. Her parents, especially her mother, seemed to like me but for some reason objected to our association. More than once I had to hide in dark places when papa visited his daughter. Margot loved the countryside. She took me to Yosemite and Lake Tahoe and taught me to float in cool mountain lakes near Desolation Valley. We spent a week at Inverness, a few days near Mount Tamalpais, and many hours at my house on Hillegass. Margot was tall, blond, beautiful. She knew numerous country-and-western songs and sang them at home and while driving. She had wanted to study mathematics, but her parents had intervened; mathematics simply was not suitable for a woman. So she studied history and literature instead. Preparing for her exams we spent sleepless nights reading boring books by even more boring individuals. It was no use—Margot failed, despite her intelligence. She was blocked in other ways as well. As a matter of fact, one might say that Margot was a pretty mixed-up lady. Yet none of this showed in her behavior outside school or daughtership. She was witty, an excellent conversationalist, rational (much more rational than I, in fact), and very, very wise. Eventually she moved east and got married. She now gives practical and moral support to people in difficult situations. We met again in 1988; we took a long walk in the Berkeley hills and talked as if we had never been separated.

When my visiting appointment ended, the administration decided to hire me. They also applied for permanent residence for me—the famous Green Card. To get it they had to argue that nobody in the United States surpassed me in my specialty. I often asked myself why I was such a hit. My big mouth certainly played a role, but the few things I had published seem to have been even more decisive. There was my Wittgensteinian monster. I hadn't written it for publication, only to clear my mind; but Anscombe had given it to a reputable philosophical journal, and it had been accepted and had impressed some people. Then there was work in an entirely different area: a paper on von Neumann's proof and another on von Neumann's theory of measurement. Neither was very original or particularly deep, but they were read and commented upon (I even received a letter from Carl Friedrich von Weizsäcker, who had discussed the papers in his seminar). The essays I had written for the Aristotelian Society were again different, in both style and content. One was a condensed version of my thesis, which in turn was a condensed version of the discussions in the Kraft Circle. The other applied the trick I had used on Wittgenstein to Niels Bohr—a difficult and much more elusive thinker. Finally, there was a short note, in English, on the so-called paradox of analysis. Being by now familiar with academic ways—the more paper you deface, the better—I wrote a German version and sent it to *Kantstudien*. The German version says exactly the same thing as the English version, but with the parts of the argument interchanged. A philosopher, I forget who, read both papers and commented on my "development." So now I had two papers and a development—a big increase in my reputation.

During a visit to Cornell University I was offered an associate professorship with tenure. Not to be left behind, California also offered tenure. I received a Fulbright scholarship and an invitation, backed by a National Science Foundation grant, to the Minnesota Center for the Philosophy of Science. I accepted Berkeley, declined the Fulbright scholarship, asked for leave and was given it, and spent my first regular Berkeley semester in Minneapolis.

At that time the Minnesota Center was one of the foremost institutions in the field. With a resident staff and a changing group of visitors, it organized conferences in Minnesota and else-where. Almost all philosophers of science of my generation were there early in their career, and all received decisive impulses for their work. The director, Herbert Feigl, and I had become friends after meeting in Vienna. Feigl was the leading PR man of logical empiricism in the United States. Being aware of overlaps with other schools and realizing their propagandistic potential, he assembled a reader, introduced the term "analytic philosophy," and used the Center as an exchange station for scholars from all fields. He was tall, distinguished-looking, with a roving eye and a knack for short and pungent phrases. Some people, de Santillana among them, have criticized him for being repetitious and behind the times. "Er ist in seiner Entwicklung stecken geblieben" ("He's got stuck in his development"), said Popper. The charge of repetitiousness may be correct—it applies to every salesman of ideas. (It certainly applies to Popper.) The charge of backwardness, however, is pure nonsense. Feigl made important contributions to philosophy in the traditional, nonpositivistic sense. He was one of the few philosophers of science who addressed the specific problems of psychologists and psychoanalysts, and he changed the empiricist philosophy of science by combining it with a rather large dose of realism. Essays such as "De Principiis Non Disputandum . . . ?" or "Existential Hypotheses" and his many attempts to clarify the mind-body problem were at the forefront of research and continue to be influential.

I saw Feigl almost every day. We met at lunch, talked until late in the afternoon, and often went to dinner with Grover Maxwell, Paul Meehl, and assorted visitors. For some time we formed a philosophical road show: Feigl represented the voice of reason while I defended more outlandish views. Having attacked each other before the astonished audience, we collected our fee, went to a restaurant, and had a good time. Even my dreams contributed to our debates. Feigl believed in incorrigible statements. He said—

what seemed to be obvious anyway—that being in pain he knew directly and with certainty that he was in pain. I didn't believe him, but had only general objections to offer. One night, however, I dreamed that I had a rather pleasant sensation in my right leg. The sensation increased in intensity, and I began to wake up. It grew even more intense. I woke up more fully and discovered that it had been a severe pain all the time. *The sensation itself told me* that it had been a sensation of immense pain, which I had mistaken for a sensation of pleasure. My German contribution to a festschrift for Viktor Kraft (title: "Das Problem der Existenz theoretischer Entitäten") reflects the twists and turns of our discussions about reality.

Grover Maxwell, the second in command at the Minnesota Center, had started as an industrial chemist. Switching to philosophy, he became a student at an age when others are already secure in a well-paid job, and yet he worked his way to the very top of his profession. He added an interesting and much-needed perspective to an enterprise that so far had used physics as its paradigm of science. Grover came from Tennessee. He spoke slowly and haltingly with a grim look on his face. I often thought he was about to hit me—but that was his friendly expression. Eventually he became Feigl's successor. He died much too soon.

Hill, a theoretical physicist, showed that most of the examples philosophers of science used to support their views were chimeras. Classical mechanics by no means "followed from" quantum mechanics for small values of Planck's constant; the theory of elasticity was anything but an extension of classical point mechanics; point mechanics, in turn, was not a simple thing but a collection of different approaches; and so on. Today these things are well known. In the fifties, not even scientists were aware of them.

Paul Meehl was interested in the mind-body problem and in the relation between theory and experiment. The positivists fa-

vored an "upward seepage" of meaning, as Meehl called it: observation statements (which we put at the bottom of our diagrams)
are meaningful; theoretical statements, taken by themselves, are
not but receive meaning via the logical links that tie them to observation statements. Continuing the drift of my 1958 paper I argued that meanings travel in the opposite direction. Sense-data in
and for themselves have no meaning; they just are. A person who
is given sense-data and nothing else is completely disoriented.
Meaning comes from ideas. Meaning, therefore, "trickles down"
from the theoretical level toward the level of observation. Today I
would say that both positions are rather naive. Meaning is not lo-
cated anywhere. It does not guide our actions (thoughts, observations) but arises in their course. Meaning may stabilize to such an
extent that the assumption of a location starts making sense. This,
however, is a disease and not a foundation.

I often returned to the Minnesota Center, sometimes for a semester, on other occasions for a week or even a day, when on my
way to the East Coast or Europe.

In 1960 I finally started lecturing at the University of California, in Berkeley. On weekends and during vacations I traveled
south to Santa Barbara, San Bernardino, Pomona College, the
University of Southern California, and the University of California at Los Angeles, and east to Boston and Pittsburgh. Tarski,
Mostovsky, and Carnap listened to a talk I gave at UCLA. After the
discussion, Carnap approached me. "I was afraid of meeting you,"
he said; "I thought you were a nasty person—but the moment you
entered the lecture hall I realized you were not." It took me some
time to find the reason for this extraordinary statement. In 1957,
after my first visit to the Minnesota Center, I had started corre-
sponding with Feigl. My letters were of a personal nature but contained irreverent comments on things I had read, Carnap's papers
included. What I did not know was that every letter that had even
the slightest intellectual content was at once copied and sent to

the persons commented upon. They wrote replies, which were again copied and sent around. Not knowing who had written the replies, I countered even more aggressively. Naturally Carnap thought I was a pain.

After my talk, Carnap invited me to dinner. "Let's talk about personal matters," he suggested; "an intellectual debate at this late hour would give me a sleepless night." Next day he drove me to the airport, or, rather, his wife drove while he kept me company in the back seat. He talked about psychoanalysis. "I once was rather critical of it," he said; "but now that I have had some personal experience I think it is not completely without content." I met Carnap again in 1964, in Alpbach. That year Feigl and I were running a joint seminar. We heard that Carnap had arrived. How can that be possible? we asked ourselves. In Los Angeles, Carnap had been rather dependent on his wife; he couldn't even get out of his chair without her help. We also knew that Ina had died, and we wondered how Carnap was getting along. He was perfectly all right, in an excellent mood, and more than ready to participate in our debates. He congratulated me after one of my presentations. I was not convinced it had been that good. "You can trust me," Carnap said. "I know about clarity." Later, at a monster debate about epistemology, I compared Aristotle's philosophy with that of the Vienna Circle. Aristotle's philosophy, I said, was fruitful—it had helped him to found some sciences and to enrich others. Ernst Mach was still making contributions to the sciences themselves, not only to the rhetoric about them. The Vienna Circle, however, merely commented on work already done. It was barren, from a scientific point of view. Or, as Ernst Bloch had colorfully put it, "Die Philosophie ist aus einer Fackelträgerin der Wissenschaft zu ihrer Schleppenträgerin geworden" ("Having been the torchbearer of science, philosophy is now carrying its train"). Carnap did not object, but he emphasized the advantages of clarity. He was a wonderful person, gentle, understanding, not at all as dry as

would appear from some (not all) of his writings and from his reputation as a superlogician.

During the following twenty years I married (for the third time); resumed singing (with Ina Souez, one of Fritz Busch's Glyndebourne stars; later, when Ina moved to Los Angeles, I flew there once a week); acquired and lost a medium-sized reputation in the philosophy of science; got jobs (permanent professorships or chairs) in Auckland, Berlin, London, Yale, Sussex, and Kassel, stayed a few months, and then resigned. I ran into the student revolution in Berkeley, London, and Berlin; became a special lecturer for the Council of Philosophical Studies in Stanford; and bought a dog. I saw Gobbi as Scarpia; Jack Rance as Boccanegra (a fantastic performance of an extremely difficult part), Nabucco, and Iago; Sutherland as Lucia and in a recital; Schwarzkopf at a recital ("she sings as if she were receiving visitors in her boudoir," I said to Barbara) and in *Così*. I visited the famous Doctor Moses, who, in addition to treating the fears and indispositions of leading singers with medicine, drinks, and lies, was now also taking care of me; and I ran into my first Busby Berkeley, during a performance of the Cockettes, a San Francisco–based transvestite group.

A screen was lowered onto the stage, and the lights were turned out. The screen is dark and a song is heard in the distance. A small dot of light appears, grows, becomes a human face, singing. The face increases in size, leans back, disintegrates; the parts reassemble and we are on Broadway. A clock shows the time. People come home from work, feed their pets, go to bed; others are getting up for the day, dress, eat, depart—there are the streets, the traffic, the workplaces. The singer returns, and we are in a nightclub. The guests converse, drink, dance. The dancing increases in speed, more dancers join, now even the floor starts moving—it's growing dark, the camera moves up, there is the clock again, people coming home from work, going to bed; the walls of their houses disintegrate, reassemble; the face reappears, moves away, becomes smaller, still smaller, only a point of light is left, now the light is gone too, the final bars of the song and—it's over. "What was that?" I exclaimed. "That was Busby Berkeley," said Mara—the Lullaby of Broadway from the Golddiggers of 1935 with Wini Shaw. What an extraordinary talent! From then on I tried to see every movie Berkeley had ever made. I regularly visited a cinema on Telegraph Avenue that showed movies from the thirties and forties. Once, in Auckland, New Zealand, I sat through an entire film festival—three days, seven hours a day. "We," that is, Robin, who started out as my teaching assistant and then became a life-long friend, and his entourage (girls, boys, dogs—but mainly girls), went to many other events, All Star wrestling included. I knew wrestling from TV. The real thing, in the Cow Palace, was like a revival meeting. Even from the distance you could hear the roaring of the crowd. Little old ladies threw their knitting into the ring: "Kill him! Kill him!" Married couples drove up in their Buicks or their Fords; they would look straight ahead when they arrived, straight ahead during the first few minutes; then gradually they melted, became attentive, raised their fists in unison, smiled at each other, and may have had the first real contact in weeks. Like everybody else I had my heroes; I trembled when they got into trouble and was relieved when they won. In Hawaii, where Robin had a job and where I stopped on my way to New Zealand, I met some of them in person. But then Robin convinced me, by word and demonstration, that it was all a fake: the outcome was predetermined, the blood artificial. I still have not forgiven him.

I gave two standard lectures, one on general philosophy, the other on the philosophy of science. I also ran a seminar in which I would invite the participants to expound their own ideas. That was not the customary way of doing things. Most of my colleagues turned seminars into means for spreading their views or the views of the school to which they belonged. The topic and long reading lists were published in advance. Not everybody could participate, and those who did had to work on well-defined projects. I preferred a more informal procedure. Some seminars were excellent, others were the pits. Occasionally I specified a topic. Once it was Aristotle. Burnyeat was there and seemed to be enjoying himself. A few years later it was Plato's *Theaetetus*. I gave a general introduction and spoke at length about Plato's theory of vision. This time Gregory Vlastos attended and seemed impressed. Still, I didn't like big shots in my seminars—they always made me feel silly. They took ideas seriously while I just tried to get things over with.

I hardly ever prepared my lectures; I made a few notes and expected rhetoric to carry me through. The method had worked on my lecture trips. But filling space with noise for an entire semester was a different matter. "How do you do it?" Robin asked; "three times, in three lectures, you say exactly the same things. Even the jokes are the same. Yet the students sit there with their mouths wide open and listen as if it were revelation." I often told the students to go home—the official notes would contain everything they needed. As a result an audience of 300, 500, even 1,200 shrank to 50 or 30. I wasn't happy about that; I would have preferred a larger audience, and yet I repeated my advice until the administration intervened. Why did I do it? Was it because I disliked the examination system, which blurred the line between thought and routine? Was it because I despised the idea that knowledge was a skill that had to be acquired and stabilized by rigorous training? Or was it because I didn't think much of my own performance? All these factors may have played a role. They faded away, and I changed gears in 1975 when, for some reason never identified by physicians, I became so weak that I could hardly stand on my feet. Now I started to prepare my classes, wrote the main points out in longhand, came to all the sessions (I had missed about a third of them while still healthy), and told some excellent and entirely novel stories.

During the days of the so-called student revolution I discussed the philosophies that had accompanied earlier revolutionary movements. Cohn-Bendit, Lenin's "Left Wing Communism—an Infantile Disorder," essays by Chairman Mao, and Mill's "On Liberty" were on my reading list. I asked students to give talks or prepare demonstrations instead of writing papers, and I invited outsiders to present their points of view. In the seminar, a student who had blown up transformers explained why. "Who is not for me is against me!" he shouted. During one of my lectures a black man, Nehemiah Pitts, said, "You white people are not even human!" We surrounded him afterward—"we" meaning students, teaching assistants, and I; we didn't argue, we just talked. Like many people, some of them famous (Lenny Bruce, for example, or Artaud), Pitts seemed to be under tremendous pressure, caused by a situation that was inhuman indeed. More black people turned up in my classes (many more, percentagewise, than are on campus today), and I was often at a loss. Should I continue feeding them the intellectual delicacies that were part of the white culture? I was a teacher, a professor even; I had accumulated information about all sorts of things and had strong opinions on a variety of topics and little respect for the leading lights of my profession. But now I felt ignorant and out of place. A black woman, handsome and powerful, invited me to her home and her family. "Be careful," she said. "My daughter can spot a fake in no time." I declined. I wish I could have explained to her that my reason was not conceit but shyness. I understood why the students welcomed Huey Newton, Bobby Seale, and their followers as if they were gods. Malcolm X came and gave a well-reasoned speech. He was dressed like a businessman, orderly, with a briefcase containing his papers. I read his *Autobiography* (written by Alex Haley, who later wrote *Roots*). I felt sympathy, even love, and an urge to contribute, though minimally, to the life of this extraordinary human being.

Responding to my invitation, Vietnamese students explained

the history of their country and the reasons for resistance. A group
of gays described how it felt living as a minority among ignorant
and confident straight people. Jan Kott, whose *Shakespeare Our
Contemporary* had been on my reading list for years, produced Eu-
ripides' *Orestes*. Orestes and Pylades appeared on motorcycles,
Menelaus was a general, Tyndareus a southern politician, and
Helen—well, Helen was a common whore. "He must have changed
many lines," I said to Alan, who had supervised the production.
"He didn't change a single line," Alan replied. And yet all the parts
fitted perfectly, as if the play had been written today. Kott, Alan,
and I also went to San Francisco to see a performance in the
Haight-Ashbury district. Kott was like a child. He was interested in
everything and treated the most common events as if they were
messages from Mars.

My friend Joan McKenna, a bigmouth with a heart of gold and
a certified witch, tried an experiment. Having been introduced as
a guest lecturer she talked for about twenty minutes; then she
stopped and invited questions. Her answers were unfair, sarcastic,
authoritarian. Nobody intervened. On the contrary, people next
to her victims moved away a little—we don't want to have anything to do with a loser like you, they seemed to say. Now Joan
explained the setup and its purpose. "Look at what you are doing!" she exclaimed. "I give ridiculous, authoritarian answers. You
not only swallow them but treat the only students brave enough
to resist like outcasts. No wonder a professor can get away with
anything!" After that we discussed how to deal with the bastards
of the profession. Assume one such superior being says things that
sound silly or incomprehensible. What do you do? You get up and
ask for clarification. Assume you are silenced by an authoritarian
gesture. Well, somebody else gets up and repeats the question: "I
didn't understand either." More anger, more sarcasm. A third student gets up: "You are supposed to teach, not to make fun of us; so
please explain." "Don't be insolent!" "He wasn't being insolent,"

a fourth student says. "He was asking for information, and you wouldn't give it"—and so on. Sooner or later, I said, there will be a more accommodating response. "We can't do that," some students replied; "we'll get bad grades." "We won't do it" was the reaction of others. "It's not worth the effort."

The students who participated in the Free Speech Movement wanted to change all that. They wanted to turn the university from a knowledge factory (that's what Clark Kerr, the president, had called it) into a community and an instrument for social improvement. Their actions affected the most timid individuals. They lit up, then started talking, and it became clear that everybody had ideas that were interesting and worthwhile. It was a tremendous achievement when the faculty supported the position of the student leaders and forced the administration to withdraw. The movement, apparently, had reached its aim. "Don't go home yet!" said Mario Savio, one of the student leaders and an excellent speaker; "we still have the Vietnam War to deal with." Now the movement changed direction and became more aggressive. Blacks from Oakland joined, gave speeches on campus, told white students about their lives. Anti–Vietnam War demonstrations began all over the country. But in California, Ronald Reagan put an end to reforms. In a way the revolutionaries had contributed to his success. Being concerned with their own problems, showing a healthy contempt for the white middle class, which in many cases included their parents and relatives, and shouting obscenities instead of explanations when confronted by TV cameras, they alienated large groups of voters. Needless to say, Reagan made the most of it.

Two weeks ago I saw a movie made in 1990 from newsreels, local reports, and the recollections of some participants in the Free Speech movement. Susan Griffin, a leading feminist, wrote part of the text and did some of the narration. It is an exciting but also a very saddening document. The enthusiasm, the hope for a new kind of academy, has long disappeared and has been replaced by lethargy, a concern about grades, and a fear of the future.

I didn't always accept the advice of the student leaders. For example, I didn't participate in the strikes they declared. On the contrary, I cut fewer lectures during the strike than either before or after. "Didn't you feel any solidarity?" Grazia asked when I told her. "With the students, yes; with the organizers of the strike, no. They presumed to speak for all students just as Johnson presumed to act for all Americans—the old authoritarianism again." Besides, I thought a student strike was rather silly. Industrial strikes cause a shortage of goods. Student strikes are a nuisance, nothing more. (I have changed my mind since then. Professors without students are as useless as screwdrivers without screws—and they feel it.) I would have stopped lecturing if my students had demanded it, but when I asked them, some said yes, some said no—and we spent the rest of the time debating the issue. Eventually I moved off campus, first into students' quarters, then into a church. Now the administration got on my back: teachers were supposed to remain in the assigned lecture halls. Consulting the regulations I found no such rule, and continued as before. For some of my colleagues, John Searle especially, this was the last straw; they wanted to have me fired. When they realized how much paperwork was involved, they gave up. Red tape does have its advantages.

11   London, Berlin, and New Zealand

In the late sixties I was still highly marketable. I received offers from London (a chair in the history and philosophy of science), Berlin (a new chair in the philosophy of science), Yale (a professorship in the philosophy of science), Auckland, New Zealand (a professorship—or was it a chair?—in the philosophy of science). I was invited to become a fellow of All Souls College, Oxford, and had an extended correspondence with the economist and philosopher Friedrich von Hayek about a possible job in Freiburg, Germany. I accepted the first three offers and declined the rest. I was already spending one term in Berkeley, one in London, again a term in Berkeley, and so on. While in London I would also work in Berlin, commuting by plane once a week. In 1968 I interpolated a semester at Yale. During the northern summer I went to Auckland for the winter semester. I even considered an offer from Georgia Tech in Atlanta. I talked about witches, inspected possible living quarters, and moved on to London. For a change I said no.

Berkeley operated year-round, so with a little cutting at the edges I could be everywhere. I had resigned from Berkeley in 1968, packed my books, arranged for them to be sent to London, handed my apartment over to Barbara, and left for Minneapolis. It had been warm and sunny in Berkeley; it was cold and damp in Minneapolis. I stayed in my hotel room and watched TV. In *Pal Joey* I spotted a section of Bay Street that I knew very well: it was the place where I took my singing lessons. Homesick, I asked Berkeley to take me back and was reappointed. Then, having phoned San Francisco Pier and asked them to hold my belongings, I moved to Boston and on to London. The provost of the University of London, Sir Ifor Evans, agreed to postpone the final decision about the chair—which started the schedule I have just described.

In London I stayed at the Georgian Hotel in Gower Street. I had a small room with a basin, lit by a bulb hanging from a wire. The toilet was downstairs, the shower the next floor up. An acquaintance to whom I had lent some money occasionally showed the place to his friends: "Here lives the guy who is financing my stay at the Dorchester."

I lectured at University College once a week, from six to eight, and at the London School of Economics. For a change, I prepared my lectures, which consisted mostly of case studies from the history of electrodynamics, optics, and quantum theory. I also repeated the story of the Copernican revolution that I had told at Berkeley. "Science has many holes," I said in passing. "A Popperian triviality," shouted Imre Lakatos, who came to every lecture. That shut me up; but I soon smiled at the incident. Lakatos had used a familiar trick: assuming that your audience does not know too much history, you can increase the stature of a modern midget by burdening him with age-old discoveries. In the present case the ancestors were clear—they were the ancient skeptics. Unfortunately this only occurred to me hours after the lecture.

The lecture hall at the London School of Economics was directly opposite Imre's office window. In spring and summer, when the windows were open, Imre could hear every word I said. Feeling outraged, or simulating outrage at the drift of my story—with Imre you were never sure—he left the Great Thinkers who happened to be with him, came over, and tried to set things right. I read the first version of my pro/anti-Kuhn paper in Popper's seminar with Popper in the chair ("Don't be too hard on Kuhn," he said) and chaired another meeting where Imre introduced an early version of his "Methodology of Scientific Research Programmes."

Imre was a rationalist of sorts—at least that was how he presented himself, as a crusader for reason, law, and order. He traveled all over the world trying to encourage doubtful rationalists and to recommend his methodology as a nostrum. On one of his trips— he had just visited Hans Jensen, a favorite target of Berkeley student radicals—he stopped at my place in the Berkeley hills. He was accompanied by Spiro Latsis, who is now an international shipping magnate and who at the time was writing his thesis with Imre. Latsis sat down in a corner and started caressing some worry beads. "Is that how you survive this business?" I asked. He only smiled. Imre invited me to come along to Stanford—lots of Important People were on his list. "Why should I?" I replied. "I know exactly what's going to happen. First you'll sip a little tea; then you'll find people both you and your host despise, and having warmed to each other in this wonderful fashion, you'll start talking about the best ways of upholding reason, law, and order." Imre did not restrict his efforts to potential converts, however. He wanted to start a general debate about the merits of rationalism. He visited almost every major history or philosophy of science conference; again he asked me to accompany him. "I can sleep at home," I replied, "and much more comfortably." "You were right," Imre wrote when the meetings were over; "a bunch of boring incompetents."

When in London, I visited Imre as a matter of course, first in a small apartment in Hampstead, right above the actor Alastair Sim, then in his luxurious house in Turner Woods. Imre had bought the house for representational purposes. It contained a kitchen, bathrooms, a large sitting room, and Imre's library on the upper floor. Visitors were first shown the garden, then fed, and finally led upstairs for serious talk. I was often invited as an extra guest. I enjoyed the garden and the dinner, but, anticipating the drift of the conversation (see above), I remained in the kitchen and helped Gillian with the dishes. Some of the guests didn't know what to make of this. Men, especially scholars, were supposed to engage in debate, while dishes were the domain of women. "Don't worry," said Imre; "Paul's an anarchist." Once we went to the theater—Imre, his girlfriend, Tarski, and I. To the Old Vic, no less. The play was a crashing bore. In the interval I invited everybody to come with me and see *Cat Ballou* with Jane Fonda and Lee Marvin. Imre was scandalized; "Paul, you are impossible," he said; "we leave a classic to see such trash." "But I liked it," Tarski said afterward.

Imre and I exchanged many letters about our affairs, ailments, aggravations, and the most recent idiocies of our dear colleagues. We differed in outlook, character, and ambition; yet we became really good friends. I was devastated and quite angry when I heard that Imre had died. "How can you do that to me?" I shouted at his shade. Cambridge University Press wanted to publish our letters, but could not: as usual I had thrown away Imre's part of the correspondence. Only a few postcards survived as bookmarks, or to cover holes in the walls of my house. I always felt that Imre's rationalism was not a matter of personal conviction but a political instrument that he would use or put aside as the situation demanded. He did have a sense of perspective. He genuinely admired Popper and wanted to form a movement around Popper's philosophy. Eventually he became disillusioned. "What has Popper done over and above Duhem?" he wrote on one of his last postcards. "Nothing." I still miss this outrageous, sensitive, ruthless, self-mocking but very humane individual.

I saw almost every theatrical production and every movie that appeared. On weekends I started in the afternoon. First a movie, then a matinee, then an evening performance, and a midnight movie after that. Once, just back from Berlin, I went to the Shafts-

bury Theatre to see *Hair*. It was an astonishing show. I felt especially attracted to a vivacious brunette who danced up a storm. I
met her next day. Daniel Revenaugh—pianist, conductor, Busoni
scholar, man about town, and my neighbor in Berkeley—had
picked her up on the way to our luncheon date. She was Rohan
McCullough, daughter of the famous Colonel McCullough whose
radio interviews during the war were already a legend. I occasionally waited for her at the stage door. We would talk briefly, and
then she was off to one of her many parties. About two years later,
when feeling bored in Imre's library, I gave her a call. From then on
we met more frequently; we went to concerts, movies, the theater,
and operatic performances. When about to leave London, I received a message from Revenaugh; he needed my house in Berkeley to solidify an affair of his own and offered a sizable sum if I
would stay away. "Well," I said to myself, "it's time for a change,"
and moved to Blakes Hotel in Roland Gardens in Kensington, my
headquarters during the next few years. I saw Rohan in Berkeley,
where she performed with the San Francisco Symphony, and in
Zurich, where she played Nerissa in an Old Vic production of *The
Merchant of Venice*. Since then we have met only once, but the love
and the friendship remain.

In Berlin I had two secretaries, one for German, one for English and French, and fourteen assistants. That posed a problem.
All my life I had been independent. Professorship had not changed
this habit. I still wrote and mailed all my own letters, including
official ones, and I certainly wrote all my books and articles from
the first draft to the final copy. I never had a mailing list or a list of
my publications, and I threw away most of the offprints that were
sent to me. That took me out of the academic landscape, but it also
simplified my life. In Switzerland, where I worked for over ten
years, I didn't even have an office. "Your stature is going to suffer,"
said some of my colleagues. I saw things differently—no office, no
office hours, no waste of time. Now I had a large room with an im-

pressive desk and antique chairs, as well as an anteroom and a secretary in it. It gave me the willies—but not for long. The secretaries were soon used by my less independent colleagues and by the assistants. "Look," I said to them, "I was given 80,000 marks for starting a new library; go and buy all the books you want and run as many seminars as you like. Don't ask me—be independent!" Most of the assistants were revolutionaries, and two of them were sought by the police. Yet they didn't buy Che Guevara, or Mao, or Lenin; they bought books on logic! "We have to learn how to think," they said, as if logic has anything to do with *that*.

The lecture hall at the University of Berlin was below street level; it was framed by glass windows and watched by armed soldiers outside. I felt like a fish in a well-protected aquarium. When the discussion turned to politics, I withdrew to the audience; "I have my prejudices," I said; "Let one of you take the chair." It was the politically correct move (and, as far as I was concerned, also the least strenuous one), but it ruined the debate; I was soon asked to return to the podium. Before class I bought beer (or coffee) and sandwiches (or sweets) for everyone and had the load delivered by the assistants. The only people with whom I had some closer contact were Jacob Taubes, an intelligent, kind, but unhappy member of the faculty; Margherita von Brentano; and Gretta Harden, an opera singer I had met in San Francisco.

I saw *Don Giovanni* and *Tales of Hoffmann* at Felsenstein's Komische Oper, and *Coriolanus* and *Arturo Ui* by the Brecht ensemble. Felsenstein seemed to think he was producing the "real" Offenbach. He had restored the spoken passages, replaced (in the German text) the mirror by the original diamond (in German, "Scintille diamant" becomes "Leuchte heller Spiegel mir," and the aria is called the "Spiegelarie"), thus clarifying, he believed, the implied reference to capitalism; and he turned Hoffmann into a pure poet unable to survive in a greedy world. This, at least, is what he wrote in the program notes. On stage I saw just another Hoffmann, drunk as usual, interesting, yes, but not especially earth-shaking. The *Don Giovanni* was a different matter. Felsenstein's approach has by now become commonplace: orchestral passages don't paralyze the action, they add to it. An entire play, detailed and well articulated, preceded Elvira's entrance in the second scene: Giovanni and Leporello have a look, then withdraw; in come servants with umbrellas, suitcases, hatboxes; they lose control of their load—a suitcase opens and spills its contents; the majordomo asks the heavens for support, fires the guilty servant, repacks the suitcase with his own majordomal hands while the rest look on in amazement; he chases them back to their work, and now at last comes Donna Elvira, elegant, slightly annoyed, with a supercilious air. It was incredible how much could be stuffed into those few bars. Elvira remains annoyed during the beginning of Leporello's aria—she doesn't want to be bothered with trivia, and by a mere servant at that; slowly, very slowly, it dawns on her what it all means; she is astonished, incredulous, devastated. Many actresses have copied the sequence, but not as effectively as I saw it done long ago in Felsenstein's production. *Il mio tesoro* became the crowing of a cock—this at least was my impression. The acting was excellent throughout, the singing adequate, which means perfectly adapted to the action.

I had never liked *Arturo Ui*; the humor is crude, the action absurd without touching the real absurdity of the times. But Ekkehard Schall's acting transcended most of these imperfections. *Coriolanus*, on the other hand, was a revelation, the fight between Coriolanus and Aufidius reduced to a quarrel between two overgrown kids, ridiculous—except for the lives it cost. The battle scenes set the whole stage in motion as if the earth was about to burst asunder, and in the midst of it was Calpurnia, ice-cold, calculating, wonderfully played by Helene Weigl. I saw the play a second time, in London. It had lost none of its power.

I don't know what prompted me to go to Yale. True, I had been invited and offered a full professorship, but why did I accept? It was a waste of time. I gave a lecture course (the same as at Berkeley) and a seminar. The seminar was attended by Jeffrey Bub, who had just started publishing on hidden variables, and a group of confused and, I'm sorry to say, whining sociologists. I was bored to tears. "It's your own fault," said my friends. "First you denigrate reason, then you expect people to say something interesting." I saw things differently. I never "denigrated reason," whatever that is, only some petrified and tyrannical versions of it. Nor did I assume that my critique was the end of the matter. It was a beginning, a very difficult beginning—of what? Of a better understanding of the sciences, better societal arrangements, better relations between individuals, a better theater, better movies, and so on. Artaud heaped scorn on the establishment, on language even, and yet he suggested new forms that have inspired playwrights, producers, philosophers, up to the present day. The people I met at Yale, however, seemed to lack any positive ideas of their own. With few exceptions they agreed with my critique; instead of moving on, however, they sat on it and bathed it in their tears. Still, I looked for a house and made a down payment on one in Branford, near New Haven. At the end of the semester I finally had had it. I resigned, picked up the down payment, and returned to Berkeley. The Yale administration who had tried so hard to catch me was very happy to see me go.

I went to Auckland twice, in 1972 and 1974. The university had established a chair, for which I had applied and had been accepted. This time I had excellent reasons: I wanted to get away from the northern pollution. I was more careful than before: I kept my Berkeley job and simply added Auckland to it. I enjoyed the scenery and the people; I even enjoyed my job. I had an apartment on campus. Waking up in the morning I heard the students going to class; sunning myself on the balcony at noon I saw them returning. The library was just a few steps away. I spent many hours there, looking at books and making notes. There were chipmunks on the roof and a tuibird in the trees nearby. It took me a long time to realize that the screeching sounds that filled the air and the flutelike tones that followed came from the same source. Looking at the night sky made me dizzy: instead of jumping forward, Leo was lying on his back. Returning via Hawaii I noticed an interesting phenomenon. Berkeley certainly was less hectic than the East—that was another reason why I had dropped Yale—and Hawaii was more peaceful still. But starting out from Auckland, the sequence was inverted. Compared with New Zealand, Berkeley seemed like a madhouse.

Nineteen seventy-four was less tranquil. I fell in love with a Canadian lady who had been a model in Europe and was now using her earnings to study philosophy. I had a foreboding when I saw her in my seminar. She was beautiful, intelligent, with a boyish body and, it turned out, no limits to her lovemaking. When I left Auckland, I promised to return in summer (winter in the northern hemisphere). In Sussex, a place I had added after hesitation time in London had come to an end, I fell ill; I grew so tired I could hardly stand on my feet. Rohan recommended her healer, Benno, a Hungarian Jew with a hunchback. Benno did not take me on at once—he had to make sure that I would respond to his treatment. After giving me a massage, he suggested some dietary measures and tested the effect. "Somebody in heaven is helping you," he said, and accepted me. The treatment consisted of extended massages, monitored by pulse and blood pressure measurement, dietary suggestions, and foot care. For the massage, Benno used an oil with special ingredients—they were supposed to absorb the impurities of my blood. And, indeed, my eyes became clearer than they had ever been before. Benno was lonely, a mixture of hatred and helplessness. "Few people are worth the effort; they have no sense of gratitude," he said, massaging a sick dog. "Animals are different." "The best thing would be to kill all Chinese," he said on another occasion; "just kill them, all of them." "Yesterday my sister visited me," he told me one day. "She died long ago. But yesterday the doorbell rang, there was a woman, she looked at me and walked away. It was my sister." Benno seemed to like me. He could speak German with me and could make sarcastic remarks about those Britons who had no sense of culture; besides, he seemed to notice the vast amounts of fear I carried around with me. I soon felt much better. I needed it. I had a shock when Judith wrote that she had started an affair. That was not my usual reaction. As far as I was concerned, love was a gift, freely exchanged, and not a bond based on a contract or on promises. But I was caught unawares. I remember leaving the university building in Falmer, Sussex, breathing the cool air and saying to myself: I am a human being, not a bag of jelly, and I shall prevail.

Although I had a tight schedule, I still had time for extras. I went to Salzburg in 1964, to Bellagio in 1966, to a huge meeting of the American Association for the Advancement of Science in Chicago in 1970, and to individual lectures in Minneapolis, Pittsburgh, Delaware, and elsewhere. Lorenzen, whom I met in Salzburg, seemed to agree with my views. He certainly liked to talk. "I bet," I said to him in front of the tape recorder that had immortalized our discussion, "wherever I turn on this tape, it will be you speaking." "No way," said Lorenzen. I spun the tape, stopped and started the machine. No Lorenzen. "You see!" Lorenzen said triumphantly. I spun it again. Again no Lorenzen. "I was right," said Lorenzen, already with a catch in his voice. When the third trial failed, Lorenzen became really concerned. I spent a wonderful week in Bellagio with von Hayek, whom I knew from Alpbach, the historian Butterfield, who was one of the resident scholars, and the writer Robert Ardrey, who became a close friend. Ardrey was one of the leftist intellectuals who had entered literature in the thirties. At that time he had two plays on Broadway in the same week, one directed by Elia Kazan. Both failed. He moved to Hollywood and wrote screenplays (*Khartoum,* for example). Being interested in human nature, he went to Africa, where the anthropologist Raymond Dart had just made some surprising announcements about human origins. Ardrey followed the debate and wrote *African Genesis,* an interesting documentation of the way in which scientists turn opinion into truth. The book is scientific in the sense that it is critical and comprehensive. But it was also written with a journalist's skepticism, not with a scientist's conceit.

After Bellagio the neurophysiologist Jung drove me to Freiburg. We saw Nietzsche's house in Sils Maria and other historical sites. Jung's wife was a huge, kind, but rather pushy woman, and Jung obeyed her most of the time. Being interested in my case—after all, I had sizable neurological problems—he invited me to his office. I had difficulty getting into the institute, for the porter couldn't believe that I, who looked like a bum, had an appointment with the "Herr Professor." I had even more trouble with the secretaries, who seemed to be in awe of the "Herr Professor." At long last the door to his office opened, and there he was, a little man behind an immense desk, waiting to take care of me.

Jung also wanted me to meet Heidegger, who occasionally came over for lunch. "However," he said, "you must put a brake on your sarcasm"—or words to that effect. I declined. That year I taught summer session in Berkeley—an hour each day for six weeks. Having chosen the history of church dogma as my subject, I read all the relevant books I could lay hands on, Harnack especially. His work does not yet appear to have been superseded. Sometimes I was one hour ahead of my class, sometimes only half an hour, sometimes two. Why church dogma? Because the development of church dogma shares many features with the development of scientific thought. I even found time to break a leg and to have a kidney stone. I led a full life. Yet on May 10, 1967, I wrote in my notebook: "So one day passes after another and it is not clear why one should live." Sentiments such as this have been faithful companions in my adventures.

12   Against Method

In the late sixties New Left Books wanted to publish a collection of my papers. "Why don't you write up the stuff you are telling your poor students?" suggested Imre. "I shall reply, and we'll have lots of fun. Personally," he added, "I would have preferred Cambridge University Press; they are a large enterprise and less concerned about their reputation than a tiny business that has only just got started and is yearning for respectability." (Imre was right. New Left replaced my Berkeley colloquialisms with British understatements and omitted all the jokes. Having lost my copy of the manuscript, I had a hard time restoring the text.) "But," Imre continued, "Judith [the person who had approached me] is a nice lady; you made a promise, so the New Left it is going to be." Thus encouraged I started concocting *Against Method* (*AM*).

AM is not a book, it is a collage. It contains descriptions, analyses, arguments that I had published, in almost the same words, ten, fifteen, even twenty years earlier. The arguments for pluralism, for example, can be found in the *Delaware Studies for the Philosophy of Science* of 1963. I repeated them with some embroideries in "Problems of Empiricism" of 1965, printed in the *Pittsburgh Studies*. The observations on Galileo (dynamics and telescope) appeared first in German, then in English, as "Problems of Empiricism, Part II," again in the *Pittsburgh Studies*. In 1968 I wrote a paper with the title "Against Method," which appeared in the

Minnesota Studies in the Philosophy of Science in 1970. At the conference that preceded the publication, I suggested that theory and
observation were not independent entities linked by rules of correspondence but formed an indivisible whole. The specific arguments for that assertion came from my review of Nagel's *Structure
of Science* (*British Journal for the Philosophy of Science,* 1964); the
general background was drawn from my thesis (1951) and the
Aristotelian Society essay of 1958. The long chapter on incommensurability was the result of extended studies based mainly on
three books: Bruno Snell's *Discovery of the Mind,* Heinrich Schäfer's
Principles of Egyptian Art, and Vasco Ronchi's *Optics: The Science of
Vision.* I still remember the excitement I felt when reading Snell
on the Homeric notion of human beings. This was not a theory
formulated to bring order into material that could stand on its
own feet; it was a set of habits that pervaded everything—
language, perception, art, poetry, as well as various anticipations
of philosophical thought. Acting accordingly, the early Greeks
seemed to live in a special and self-contained world.

I had thought of such worlds for some time, though abstractly
and without examples. In 1952/53, while on my scholarship in
London, I had read Susan Stebbing's *Philosophy and the Physicists.*
Stebbing describes how a scientist and a "savage person" (that's
what members of non-Western cultures were called at the time)
see a jar. For a scientist the jar is a piece of matter made into a certain shape. For the savage it has a magical meaning defined by its
ritual function. But, says Stebbing, when the scientist and the savage look at a part of the jar's surface, *they see the same thing.* "No!" I
shouted, almost by instinct, and tried to imagine what the difference might be. I was puzzled by Anaximander's idea that the sun
and the moon were holes in dark structures containing fire. Did
Anaximander *see* the moon as a hole or was he just speculating?
According to Plutarch's *Face in the Moon,* some people interpreted
the face as a visual disturbance while for others the moon was a

glare issuing from a single luminous point. Did they perceive the moon in that manner? And is it possible for simple perceptions to vary so drastically? Often when wandering around in the country-side I stared at the silver disk, trying hard to make it appear as a hole, or a glare; I didn't succeed. Galileo's telescopic observations now became much more adventurous than Galileo had thought them to be. They not only increased knowledge; they changed its structure. The discussions in the Kraft Circle and the thesis I had written as a result had much to do with my tendency to see rup-tures where historians and even the historical actors themselves were in the habit of postulating a smooth development.

All these impressions, surprises, ideas, reinforcements lin-gered, occasionally raised their head, but seemed unacceptable when I met them in others: my contrariness extended even to ideas that resembled my own. For example, I criticized the manu-script of Kuhn's *Structure of Scientific Revolutions*, which I read around 1960, in a rather old-fashioned way. In the late sixties or early seventies I gave a public talk in Hamburg, with von Weizsäcker in the chair. In the seminar that followed I repeated my reasons for basing research on sets of conflicting theories. Both confirmation and content, I said, depend on a confrontation with alternatives (hidden variable theories in the case of quantum mechanics). Von Weizsäcker responded with a detailed account of the problems that had arisen; he showed how these problems had been attacked and solved and to what extent the new predictions had been confirmed. Compared with this rich pattern of facts, principles, explanations, frustrations, new explanations, analo-gies, predictions, etc., etc., my plea seemed thin and insubstantial. It was well enough argued, but the arguments occurred in outer space, as it were; they had no connection with scientific practice. For the first time I felt, I did not merely think about, the poverty of abstract philosophical reasoning. These, then, were some of the events that had impressed me and some of the opinions I held when I started composing my collage. I arranged them in a suitable order, added transitions, replaced moderate passages with more outrageous ones, and called the result "anarchism." I loved to shock people, and besides, Imre wanted to have a clear conflict, not just another shade of gray.

Today I am convinced that there is more to this "anarchism" than rhetoric. The world, including the world of science, is a complex and scattered entity that cannot be captured by theories and simple rules. Even as a student I had mocked the intellectual tumors grown by philosophers. I had lost patience when a debate about scientific achievements was interrupted by an attempt to "clarify," where clarification meant translation into some form of pidgin logic. "You are like medieval scholars," I had objected; "they didn't understand anything unless it was translated into Latin." My doubts increased when a reference to logic was used not just to clarify but to evade scientific problems. "We are making a logical point," the philosophers would say when the distance between their principles and the real world became rather obvious. Compared with such doubletalk, Quine's "Two Dogmas of Empiricism" was like a breath of fresh air. J. L. Austin, whom I heard in Berkeley, dissolved "philosophy" in a different way. His lectures (later published as *Sense and Sensibilia*) were simple, but quite effective. Using Ayer's *Foundations of Empirical Knowledge,* Austin invited us to read the text literally, to really pay attention to the printed words. This we did. And statements that had seemed obvious and even profound suddenly ceased to make sense. We also realized that ordinary ways of talking were more flexible and more subtle than their philosophical replacements. So there were now two types of rumors to be removed—philosophy of science and general philosophy (ethics, epistemology, etc.)—and two areas of human activity that could survive without them—science and common sense.

But that was not the end of the story. Science and common

sense are not as simple, self-contained, and faultless as the critics of their philosophical superstructures, myself included, were assuming. There is not one common sense, there are many (I argued this point with Austin but could not convince him). Nor is there one way of knowing, science; there are many such ways, and before they were ruined by Western civilization they were effective in the sense that they kept people alive and made their existence comprehensible. Science itself has conflicting parts with different strategies, results, metaphysical embroideries. It is a collage, not a system. Moreover, both historical experience and democratic principles suggest that science be kept under public control. Scientific institutions are not "objective"; neither they nor their products confront people like a rock, or a star. They often merge with other traditions, are affected by them, affect them in turn. Decisive scientific movements were inspired by philosophical and religious (or theological) sentiments. The material benefits of science are not at all obvious. There *are* great benefits, true. But there are also great disadvantages. And the role of the abstract entity "science" in the production of the benefits is anything but clear.

I greatly admire Johann Nestroy, the nineteenth-century Austrian writer of dialect comedies. His couplets, dialogues, monologues, and plays are about perfectly ordinary situations, but they present them slightly off-center. That causes laughter—another rather ordinary, "normal" occurrence. What I have found interesting in Nestroy is that the combination of normalities gradually assumes a sinister complexion. Nestroy uses extremely simple means (such as changes from dialect to high German and back to dialect again) to reveal pretense, deception, and, maybe, a basic crookedness of the entire world. I have read almost all of Nestroy's plays, not once but often, and I have seen many performances. I always felt that I was witnessing a very special phenomenon that might also be applied to scientific jargon. Karl Kraus used the phenomenon to show the incipient bestiality behind an advertisement, a newspaper article, a piece of profound reasoning. Like Austin he invited people to read literally, word for word, what was before them. Unlike Austin he found inhumanity, not just nonsense.

In a similar way the Dadaists brought sublime but inhumane thoughts down to earth and back into the sewers from which they had emerged. After destroying the language that had lent itself to such machinations, they rebuilt it, revealing what it could do when used simply and with imagination. "After their diagnosis," I wrote in *Science in a Free Society,* "the dadaistic exercises assumed another, more sinister meaning. They revealed the frightening similarity between the language of the foremost commercial travellers in 'importance,' the language of philosophers, politicians, theologians, and brute inarticulation. The praise of honor, patriotism, truth, rationality, honesty that fills our schools, pulpits, political meetings *imperceptibly merges into inarticulation* no matter how tightly it has been wrapped into literary language and no matter how hard its authors try to copy the style of the classics, and the authors themselves are in the end hardly distinguishable from a pack of grunting pigs." Following Nestroy and the Dadaists I avoided scholarly ways of presenting a view and used common locutions and the language of show business and pulp instead. (This led to problems with translators. Trained to find clear ideas behind puzzling words, and confounding ideas with frozen memories of professional slogans, they turned my text into a graveyard.)

The collage was finished in about a year. I read two sets of proofs and thought that now at last I could turn to other things. After all, I had said everything I ever wanted to say. I was very much mistaken.

So far I had debated with small groups of people, most of them personal friends. They rarely agreed with me. But they did pay attention, and their criticism was at least aimed at the right target. Reading the reviews, I faced illiteracy pure and simple for the first time. I didn't realize it right away. Having forgotten the details of my collage and being too lazy to check, I often took the critics at their word. So when a reviewer wrote "Feyerabend says X" and then attacked X, I assumed that I had indeed said X and tried to defend it. Yet in many cases I had not said X but its opposite. Didn't I care about what I had written? Yes and no. I certainly didn't feel the religious fervor some writers apply to their products; as far as I was concerned, *AM* was just a book, not holy writ. Moreover, I could be easily convinced of the merits of almost any view. Written texts, my own text included, often seemed ambiguous to me—they meant one thing, they meant another; they seemed plausible, they seemed absurd. Small wonder my defenses of *AM* confused many readers.

Most critics accused me of inconsistency: I am an anarchist, they said, but I still argue. I was astonished by this objection. A person addressing rationalists certainly can argue with them. It doesn't mean *he* believes that arguments settle a matter, *they* do. So if the arguments are valid (in their terms), they must accept the result. It was almost as if rationalists regarded argument as a sacred ritual that loses its power when used by a nonbeliever. "He says A," the critics exclaimed when I formulated a premise they accepted to produce a result they did not, "but he obviously opposes A; therefore he is inconsistent." Were philosophers really that unaware of the function of reductio ad absurdum? Some readers had difficulties with my style. They read innuendos as statements of fact and jokes as serious comments. "He whines, he splutters," said one; "He writes like Karl Kraus," said another. Everybody said I was mean and aggressive—another big surprise. True, I didn't mince words, but I certainly wasn't the raging monster that jumped at me from the reviews. Aggressive people accused me of aggression. That had happened before. "I am not going to read your diatribe!" Popper had shouted when he saw my comments on his diatribe against Bohr. (He calmed down when I told him that many people had complained about my aggressive style and had ascribed it to his influence. "Is that so?" he said, smiling, and walked away.)

Then the scientists got into the act. Some praised my plea for a less dogmatic approach, others regarded me as "the worst enemy of science" (*Nature* 1987). And why? Because I had said that approaches not tied to scientific institutions might have some value. Were such approaches unholy heresies? Scientists certainly had not always felt that way. Darwin had paid attention to animal breeders and naturalists; Descartes, Newton, Thomson, Joule, Whewell had given religious reasons for some of their most basic assumptions; scientific agents of conservation and development had learned and were still learning from local populations, while anthropologists were discovering that the objective approach they had used as a matter of course had given them caricatures; and so on.

In *AM* I also suggested that science be subjected to public control. This suggestion is not as radical as it sounds. Science is anything but the "free" and "open" enterprise philosophers are dreaming about. Business considerations play a large role, the race for Nobel Prizes drastically reduces communication between scientists, citizens' initiatives discovered problems overlooked by scientists and legitimized practices denounced by them. Testifying before the law, experts have to respond to laypersons and their representatives, that is, lawyers. True, this has led to excesses, but the fault lies in the manner of application, not in the principle. Science, it is often said, is a self-correcting process that can only be disturbed by outside interference. But since democracy is also a self-correcting process, science, being part of it, can therefore be corrected by the corrections of the larger entity.

Gradually I became acquainted with "intellectuals." They constitute a very special community. They write in a special way, have special sentiments, and seem to think of themselves as the only legitimate representatives of the human race, which in practice means other intellectuals. Intellectuals are not scientists but may rhapsodize about scientific achievement. They are not philosophers either, but they have undercover agents in that business. Thomas Nagel is one, Rorty another; even Searle turns up here and there, though he lacks the smooth ways of the true intellectual. This community now started taking a slight interest in me: it lifted me up to its own eye level, took a brief look at me, and dropped me again. After making me appear more important than I ever thought I was, it enumerated my shortcomings and put me back in my place. That really confused me.

Somewhere in the middle of the commotion I grew rather depressed. The depression stayed with me for over a year; it was like an animal, a well-defined, spatially localizable thing. I would wake up, open my eyes, listen—Is it here or isn't it? No sign of it. Perhaps it's asleep. Perhaps it will leave me alone today. Carefully, very carefully, I get out of bed. All is quiet. I go to the kitchen, start breakfast. Not a sound. TV—*Good Morning America,* David What's-his-name, a guy I can't stand. I eat and watch the guests. Slowly the food fills my stomach and gives me strength. Now a quick excursion to the bathroom, and out for my morning walk—and here she is, my faithful depression: "Did you think you could leave without me?" Yet I had often warned my students not to identify with their work. I told them, "If you want to achieve something, if you want to write a book, paint a picture, be sure that the center of your existence is somewhere else and that it's solidly grounded; only then will you be able to keep your cool and laugh at the attacks that are bound to come." I myself had followed this advice in the past, but now I was alone, sick with some unknown affliction; my private life was in a mess, and I was without a defense. I often wished I had never written that fucking book.

Confronted with a world I didn't understand but which seemed important, I started thinking that I might have "something to say," and I tried to say it in better ways. I replied to reviews, wrote two sequels to *AM,* compiled an edition of my collected papers, and planned a book that would present "my position" in a more convincing manner. Writing and rewriting tedious chapters about tedious things wasted precious time that I could have spent lying in the sun, watching television, going to the movies, or possibly even producing a few plays. It is true that before *AM* was published, I had accumulated a long list of publications, but that had been almost accidental. I loved traveling and giving talks to professional and lay audiences. I never prepared for them; I made a few notes, and adrenalin did the rest. Most of the lectures formed part of a series, which the organizers wanted to publish; so having given my speech, I had to write it down. The resulting papers earned me a full professorship, tenure, and a good salary. And that was that, as far as I was concerned. From now on, I discouraged administrators from trying to get me farther up the ladder. "You won't succeed, and I don't need it," I said; "besides, I've done with writing." (I was passed over a few times as I had wished, but forced twice to hand in "evidence of work." I was advanced both times—to my great surprise.) It was an excellent plan, but it crumbled before the assaults on *AM.*

The early critics of the book were rationalists and science freaks. Times have changed, and so have the standards of political correctness, but chauvinism, illiteracy, and intolerance are still with us. An example will show what I mean.

"Any reader of Feyerabend," writes Hilary Rose, "must see that his philosophical prescription of 'anything goes' is profoundly linked to his lewd sexist conception of a new theory as a charming courtesan whose sole purpose is his delectation. . . . It goes without saying that the 'you' who 'can do anything you like' is profoundly gendered. No one could for a moment consider that women were being invited to do anything we like."

Well, I am accustomed to weird remarks, but this one certainly takes the cake. "Is the woman nuts?" I exclaimed when reading the passage. "How on earth did she get the idea that *AM* is for males only, and even 'profoundly' so?"

Then a friend pointed out that in an earlier paper I had indeed linked good theories to courtesans. Concluding my account of a tolerant methodology, I had said that it "changes science from a stern and demanding mistress into an attractive and yielding courtesan who tries to anticipate every wish of her lover. Of course," I had continued, "it is up to us to choose either a dragon or a pussycat for our company. I do not think I need to explain my own preferences." It appears that Rose was alluding to these five lines (which appeared ten years before *AM*) when writing her comments.

Rose does not mention the article that contains these lines. In a footnote she refers to *AM* and *Science in a Free Society* as if the lines occurred in these books and characterized their outlook. Probably she has not even read the books.

I won't dwell on the fact that my remarks can be interpreted in at least two ways, serious and deadpan. But humor and irony do not seem to be Rose's strong suit. Assuming that the remarks were meant seriously, I must point out that my words can hardly be considered "lewd," except perhaps by individuals sharing the fears of the fathers of puritanism. They certainly are not "sexist." They neither say nor imply that all women are courtesans, or that it is their proper task to be courtesans, or that they have no other calling but pleasing men; that would be "sexist." They explicitly say that it is my "preference" to be served by a courtesan, which means that I shall look for a woman so inclined (there are many such women) and have fun with her just as she, being so inclined, will have fun with me. After all, I make it clear that there are other women, "stern and demanding mistress[es]," and other men who like to consort with *them*. I agree that the choosers are all males. That was intentional. The article ridicules Popperian maniacs—and there is not a single woman among those.

We are living in a time when people with particular sexual preferences are called upon to come out of the closet and efforts are being made to adapt laws and social institutions to their lifestyle. Neither gays nor lesbians say that everybody is, or has the duty to be, gay or lesbian; they say that *they* are, that there are people ready to join them, and that they want to have the right and the legal protection to live accordingly. In other words, they want to *act* on their preferences, *write about* them, and orient their *research* and their *artistic efforts* around them. Does Rose suggest that males who prefer consenting courtesans return to the closet or, even better, stop having such "lewd" desires?

Finally, even if I was indeed a male chauvinist pig when I wrote the lines, couldn't I have changed during the ten years that separate them from *AM*? And how are we going to determine *that*? By reading the book, obviously, and not by inferring its content from earlier utterances. Not everybody proceeds in this way, of course. There are organizations that judge individuals in a more holistic manner. Assuming that a soul once rotten stays rotten forever, they look for suspicious incidents and use them to mark a person for life. Examples are the Inquisition, certain Puritan communities, and the KGB—all of them conceived and run by males. Are these the people Rose wants to imitate?

I agree that for a long time men assumed a role justified neither by their intelligence nor by their character and certainly not by their achievements, and that we all, with very few exceptions, have been involved in this arrangement. Rewriting *AM* for the third edition, I was surprised to see how often I had used the male pronoun or a male phrase to refer to people in general. This may look like a small matter, but I don't think it is. Small gestures support big prejudices. The solution is not an inversion of prejudices but a wider view that includes everybody, even animals, which certainly prefer living in peace and freedom to being crowded into superfarms, often mutilated in transport, and tortured in spotless laboratories.

What do I think of *AM* today? Well, scientists have always acted in a loose and rather opportunistic way when *doing* research, though they have often spoken differently when *pontificating* about it. By now this has become a commonplace among historians of science. In analyzing Galileo's telescopic observations, I indicated how Galileo, without much theorizing, achieved authoritative reports. More recently, historians have suggested that observational levels form entire cultures, whose criteria and rules differ considerably from those of the theoreticians. And in analyzing Galileo's theoretical achievements (in connection with his defense of Copernicus—the *Two New Sciences* are a different matter), I suggested that they involved a deceptive restructuring of fundamental ideas and relations. Today such processes are being examined in considerable detail. I am far from claiming that the historians engaged in these new types of research have necessarily read *AM* and were educated by it—nothing would be further from the truth. But it is pleasant to see that some armchair views of mine are being held by scholars working in close contact with scientific practice.

Other armchair views did not fare so well. I am referring to my "relativism," to the idea that cultures are more or less closed entities with their own criteria and procedures, that they are intrinsically valuable and should not be interfered with. To a certain extent this view coincided with the views of anthropologists who, trying to understand the confusing complexity of human existence, divided it into (mostly) nonoverlapping, self-contained and self-maintaining domains. But cultures interact, they change, they have resources that go beyond their stable and objective ingredients or, rather, beyond those ingredients which at least some anthropologists have condensed into inexorable cultural rules and laws. Considering how much cultures have learned from each other and how ingeniously they have transformed the material thus assembled, I have come to the conclusion that *every culture is potentially all cultures* and that special cultural features are changeable manifestations of *a single human nature*.

This conclusion has important political consequences. It means that cultural peculiarities are not sacrosanct. There is no such thing as a "culturally authentic" suppression, or a "culturally authentic" murder. There is only suppression and murder, and both should be treated as such, with determination if necessary. Having realized the potentialities for change inherent in every culture, however, we must open ourselves to change before trying to change others. In other words, we must pay attention to the wishes, the opinions, the habits, the suggestions of the people about to be interfered with, and we must obtain our information *by way of extended personal contacts,* not from a distance, not by trying to be "objective," not by consorting with so-called leaders. Human missionaries have always followed these rules. The unwieldy and often pushy business of "development" shows clearly how much can be learned from local communities and how even the best programs fail when imposed without an attempt to understand local ways of life. At any rate, objectivism and relativism not only are untenable as philosophies, they are bad guides for a fruitful cultural collaboration. Some of my earlier writings made precisely this point, though it was a long time before I was aware of that emphasis. Thus I was not only ahead of others, I was even ahead of myself.

13   Brighton, Kassel, and Zurich

In the early seventies I considered settling down in New Zealand. The country was beautiful, the air clear, the population pleasant, and life at the university not entirely unbearable. Judith and I thought of acquiring some land and building a house. We had reasons for being optimistic. The father of a mutual friend wanted to sell part of his property along the coast, and a group of Buddhists wanted to buy. They in turn were ready to leave us five acres and to construct a house at cost; there were carpenters, electricians, plumbers, and the like among them. The project never got anywhere. Having discovered that he was dealing with Buddhists, the owner dropped the deal. "I'm not going to sell my good land to some fucking Buddhists," he is supposed to have said. I was lucky. There is no way of telling how our religious friends would have acted in the long run, and besides, Judith soon had other things on her mind.

I have no idea why and how I went to the University of Sussex at Brighton. All I remember is that I met Asa Briggs, the president, and some members of the faculty. One of them, Gallie, already knew me from the Colston symposium in Bristol. He was surprised to hear that I intended to reconstruct the original performances of well-known plays. I don't know what we agreed upon either; what I do remember is that I taught two terms (1974/75) and then resigned; twelve hours a week (one lecture course, the rest tutorials) was too much. On top of everything else, I felt weak and distracted. Some students commented upon my drawn appearance—yet the course had standing room only. I wish I could have given better lectures! In September 1974 I went to a conference in Nafplion, Greece. It had been organized by Imre Lakatos and was financed by papa Latsis. Imre had invited leading philosophers, historians (of mathematics, of the physical sciences), and economists to test the power of his program, and he intended to give a rousing introductory speech. But he died, and I gave the speech in his place, imitating his mannerisms and his ways of praising reason and vilifying irrationality. I had some trouble getting into Greece. Being in a frivolous mood I had sent a telegram: "Recovering from jaundice, a cold, and a spot of syphilis, so have a doctor ready." The telegram was intercepted, and papa Latsis had to explain me to the authorities. He seemed to enjoy the commotion.

I do remember how I got to Zurich (the famous Federal Institute of Technology, also known as the Zurich Polytechnic). It started with Erich Jantsch. Erich and I had studied astronomy in Vienna but had not seen each other for years. When we met again in Berkeley, Erich was a guru of self-organization. He was famous, respected, but without a regular job and, so it seems, without friends. He visited me rather frequently and talked to me about personal matters, scientific scandals, and new discoveries from all fields. Then he fell ill. He went to an acupuncturist and, after that, to a hospital. He was dead in a week. I didn't hear of it until I re-

ceived a document to the effect that Professor Jantsch's ashes had
been scattered over the Pacific Ocean at longitude alpha and lati-
tude beta and that the costs were "as outlined below." (I was not
the only one who received the report; at least five people paid the
full price for Erich's last rites; they are still suing.) Naturally I
wanted to know details. I rang the hospital, but the physicians
were at a loss. Yes, they knew about Erich Jantsch. He had arrived
with something like diabetes, had lingered for a while; then his
immune system had collapsed in a strange way and he had died.
This sounds like a very early case of AIDS. Erich's last friend, apart
from me, was a she-donkey. The donkey lived in a park behind my
house, and Erich had obtained permission to take her on some of
his walks. This he did twice a week, like clockwork. Occasionally
he went on lecture trips. When he returned, the lady played hard
to get. Erich had to use all his powers of persuasion, mainly sugar
and carrots, to regain her attention.

On one of his visits Erich told me in passing that the Zurich
Polytechnic was looking for a philosopher of science. "That may
be it," I said to myself. I sat down and wrote a letter to the president: "I heard you need a philosopher of science; I am interested."
It turned out that the job was still only a thought in the president's
mind, but he promised to consider me if and when it materialized.

A year later I was invited for a trial lecture, a single, two-hour
lecture on any topic whatsoever. Gerhard Huber and his wife received me and took me out to lunch. "I brought my wife along,"
Huber explained when everything was over; "she can figure a person out; I can't." It seems that I passed this first decisive test.

The lecture was set for five o'clock. By that time I was already
rather tired. Huber introduced me, and I began. There was no
chair, no table, not even a standing desk. I had to walk around during the entire lecture. That may not sound like a major problem,
but having a bum leg and being weakened by a circulatory problem I needed all my willpower to survive. I stopped after about

forty minutes. "Say something!" I exclaimed, looking at the audience. They said a lot, some of it rather aggressively. I responded in kind. One gentleman who looked like a professor accused me of trying to return to the Middle Ages. "What do you know about the Middle Ages?" I asked. "Do you know the work of Buridan, or of Oresme? How many lines of St. Thomas have you read?" He left in a rage, slamming the door behind him. Slowly, very slowly, the questions thinned out and people started leaving the lecture hall. "Over at last!" I said to myself. Not so; after the lecture (and this I did not know) I was supposed to meet the selection committee consisting of Huber, van der Waerden, Jean Hersch (a former pupil of Karl Jaspers and equally full of moral substance), the president, and others.

By now I was thoroughly fed up—and my answers showed it. "Why do you want to come to Zurich?" asked the president. "Because I'm restless and I like change." "But why Switzerland?" "Because the pay is good and the teaching load minimal." I didn't lie. Moving around from one place to another I had discovered what I really wanted: another place, apart from Berkeley, preferably Europe, with a large salary and a small teaching load. Then somebody raised the question of truth. I explained that I regarded the notion as a rhetorical device, that I intended to use it for catching flies but otherwise I didn't really take it seriously. "But even we mathematicians speak of truth," said van der Waerden. And so on. Next morning I flew to London and on to Berkeley. I was convinced that the Polytechnic wouldn't touch me with a ten-foot pole. But I had underestimated the Swiss.

To get a clearer view of me, they contacted philosophers and philosophers of science, in Berkeley and elsewhere. On my sixty-fifth birthday, Peter Schindler, then assistant to the president, sent me a selection of the replies they had received. Here are some of them:

"Feyerabend has a reputation for going from place to place."

"Apparently he likes collecting job offers."

"His at times impish penchant for a *succès de scandale* has aroused ire in some quarters."

"He has constantly been in conflict with the course committee. I am not sure whether this is a good or a bad recommendation." (This must have been somebody from Berkeley.)

"Under no circumstances would I get him to Zurich."

"If I had to decide whether to have him around either full time or not at all, I am far from sure what I would choose."

"In sum, it appears that his appointment would contribute greatly to the renown of any department of philosophy."

And so on.

Next (but still unbeknownst to me), the committee narrowed the number of applicants down to two—Scheurer, a guy from Belgium, and me. It was decided that we should give one lecture course each, for one semester. At that time I was spending part of my life in Berkeley, part in Kassel. Taking this schedule into consideration, the Polytechnic suggested that I come once every two weeks for two days and lecture for two hours each day. Surprised, I accepted. I gave my usual philosophy of science course, still without a chair or a table, wandering around and getting exhausted. Huber was there; so were Primas, van der Waerden, and other professors. One chemist, so Primas told me much later, grew angry in the first lecture, even angrier in the second, but he continued to come. Many students felt the same, both then and in other courses, and they told me so. Van der Waerden would interrupt and raise objections, and we would have a lively exchange. After the lectures I would go to my hotel (the Hotel Leoneck at the foot of the hill), lie down on the bed, and read one of the mystery stories I had bought at the railway station. I enjoyed myself. But van der Waerden was worried: "It doesn't look good for you."

Another long silence. Having abandoned Kassel I decided to remain in Berkeley and stop moving about; slowly I adapted to the American way of life. I learned to drive, bought a car and a house in the Berkeley hills, and started attending the departmental meetings I had so far avoided. Why not? I said to myself; Berkeley is my home, the university my source of income, so I might as well make the best of it.

There were other reasons as well. I preferred speaking, writing, and thinking in English (I still do). I also preferred the multiracial surroundings in Berkeley—lots of different faces, lots of ways of looking at the world. When commuting between Berlin and London I felt at home in London, not in Berlin. This was where I belonged, this was the language I wanted to speak. At that point the president of the Zurich Polytechnic invited me for another visit and made an offer: a full professorship, either full time or half time with the option of changing to full time whenever I wanted, four to five hours' teaching per week. That much I understood. What I did not understand and failed even to inquire into was that my retirement salary would be 60 percent of my full pay (I assumed it would be full pay), that I had been brought into the retirement system (others had to make a sizable contribution), and that my round trips to Berkeley would be fully paid. I accepted without even negotiating. "Do you need an office?" the president asked. "No," I said, which suited both of us. It suited the president, for there was little space available, and it suited me: no office meant no office hours. And now began ten wonderful years of half Berkeley, half Switzerland. It was exactly the situation I had been looking for.

Many years later I was told how I had landed the job. My lecture series had been a hit, numberwise—my competitor lost almost his entire audience. But many people objected to the content, and some had doubts about my character: a flippant guy like me didn't seem to be the right person for teaching a serious subject like philosophy. The federal authorities recommended rejection. The president, on the other hand, wanted to assert the independence of academic institutions, and selected me. "Even a Feyerabend can't ruin a big school like the Polytechnic," he is supposed to have said. Thus an action I had often criticized is responsible for the comfortable life I am leading today.

I found an apartment in Meilen on Lake Zurich (I'm still in it). Half the rent was paid by the school; the furniture (except for the bed) came entirely from the school (I still have it). My job was to fill at least four hours a week with talk and discussion. I solved the problem by giving one two-hour lecture and one two-hour seminar. I soon realized that the turnover in Zurich was much smaller than in Berkeley—the same people came three or four years in a row. This meant that I had to prepare at least three more lecture courses—a difficult job, but not uninteresting. When I arrived in Zurich I heard that instruction in philosophy of science was being given by a former physicist turned logician, with a precise way of thinking—Paul Hoyningen Huene. Whenever I made a sloppy remark in any of my lectures, I looked around the room for a sneer on some face: that would be him, I thought. We met at a party for his fortieth birthday; telling him that we were playing the same con game, I proposed that we start using first names. Paul has become one of my closest friends. He is an excellent cook and host, with an extensive knowledge of good wines—logicians are not so bad after all.

My first course was on Plato's dialogue *Theaetetus*. I went through the dialogue line by line with frequent asides on ancient and modern problems. For example, I connected Plato's theory of perception with quantum mechanics, and I dealt at length with his reasons for choosing the dialogue over the epic, the drama, the public speech, and the scientific essay as a means of communication. "Plato thought about his style," I said; "today the style of a scientific paper is decided by editors." I also lectured on the *Ti-*

maeus. This was difficult stuff and I was not always well prepared. Before a lecture I would often sit in a large hall watching the clock on the nearby church and growing more and more despondent: fifteen minutes to go; ten minutes to go. Shall I stay and give my lecture, or pretend to have lost my voice and run away? I gave all my lectures. "Excellent," said van der Waerden at a party he gave afterward. "What will you do next year?" "Aristotle's physics." "Ah, boring old Aristotle—I shan't come." Aristotle was more difficult than Plato and more technical. But I think his *Physics* contains material that may be of interest to modern scientists. (Gunther Stent and René Thom agree, though for vastly different reasons.)

The seminar started as in Berkeley: no set topic, but presentations by the participants. I interrupted, often after the first sentence, to get the debate going. During the third meeting a serious-looking gentleman with beard and glasses rose and read a text to the effect that there were too many interruptions and that talking a lot did not mean that one had something to say. The following week he asked me for an appointment and unfolded a plan of his own. The seminars were to be open to the general public; there was to be an overall topic for each semester to be treated by two to four "authorities" per meeting. He would do the paperwork, write the invitations, negotiate with the parties, make last-minute arrangements, and so forth. All I had to do was sign documents, give advice, introduce the guests, and occasionally give a talk myself. I accepted at once—the less I had to do, the better. Thus arose an institution that soon became very popular.

Some meetings were technical and attracted only a small audience, others had to be shown on closed-circuit TV. There was a seminar on Goethe's theory of colors. A follower of Rudolf Steiner explained Goethe's views. He had large posters with Goethe's illustrations and invited us to look at them through prisms he had handed out in advance. For the first time we *saw*, not only read or heard, what Goethe was talking about. The debate was quite lively. "You argue like an authority," a Steinerian accused Res Jost, who in the discussion had attacked some Steinerian formulations. "But I am an authority," said Jost. And so on. When the meeting was over and we moved out into the streets, we ran into elephants, camels, horses—the circus had just come to town. "A fitting conclusion to Feyerabend's seminar," wrote the *Neue Zürcher Zeitung*. Friedrich Dürrenmatt spoke on Platonic entities, using a chair instead of a bed as an example. His conclusion: the Platonic chair is nothing but the idealized hind end of the sitters. Dürrenmatt had been warned that there would be other talks and that he had to restrict himself to twenty minutes. "Oooch," he replied. "I won't know what to say anyway; I won't talk for more than ten minutes." He was late, and we started without him; when he arrived, he produced a huge manuscript and would have gone on forever if he hadn't been stopped after twenty-five minutes. (Mrs. Huber, who was chairing the meeting, hesitated to interrupt, but I, sitting next to her, egged her on: "No exceptions for big shots!") Dürrenmatt didn't say a word. He came to dinner with us afterward, tried to get me drunk, told me that he had read *Against Method,* and entertained us with stories about himself and Hohler. But he refused to come again. "You don't let a person finish!" he yelled at the organizer when he next rang him—and hung up. All in all there were seven (I believe) such seminars, held in seven consecutive years. Christian Thomas, who had criticized the original arrangement and suggested the new format, has become a very good friend.

Slowly I relaxed a little. I went to the movies, to the theater, to the opera. I took long walks in the woods and extended strolls in town. After some of the more interesting seminars I invited students and lecturers to a nearby restaurant and paid for the whole event. That cost me as much as 600 francs an evening. It didn't matter; I had an enormous salary—actually two salaries, more than enough in case I wished to retire—a house in the Berkeley hills, and a flat in Vienna, and there was no need to save. Zanussi, the by now famous Polish movie director (I was not particularly interested in him, but Irena was, so I took him along), Meret Oppenheim, Eysenck, and my old friend Tom Kuhn were among my guests. Back in Berkeley I discovered the Chez Panisse restaurant and had dinner there almost every day. My Berkeley schedule now was as follows: I rose at 6:30 (for an eight o'clock lecture—I thought nobody would come, but the lecture hall was full, as usual); office hours in one of the plazas until eleven; then home, and lunch with Perry Mason (the old series); after that either a siesta on the balcony or a little work; at five o'clock down to Chez Panisse for an early dinner; back in time for an evening show; and to bed at ten. I kept this schedule for years. In Switzerland I had lunch at home or, on Wednesdays, at school; again dinner out, either at the Luft restaurant in Meilen or in a classier place; and, after that, the evening show. Martina, whom I had met in Berkeley, came over occasionally; I visited her, in turn, in Tübingen. I owe her a lot, though I am sure she would be surprised to hear it. And slowly, very slowly, I got my intellectual act together.

This doesn't mean that having long ago decided to devote myself to intellectual matters I finally discovered the right way of doing so. I never thought of myself as an intellectual, much less as a philosopher. I practiced the trade because it gave me an income, and I continue to practice it partly out of inertia, partly because I enjoy telling stories—on paper, on TV, before a live audience. I had always liked to talk about practically anything under the sun. Though speaking with great assurance, I never felt that I was doing something special, or that I had a special calling, or that having started to interfere in philosophical matters I was bound by special loyalties. When I became first a lecturer and then a professor of philosophy, I regretted the loss of other opportunities these appointments entailed: my chances for a theatrical career were diminished. Naturally I devoted a little more attention to the business of abstract thought, which fascinated me because it affected people in such strange ways, but that didn't mean I had committed my life to it. The critical reactions to *Against Method* confused me. Leaping to the defense, I began to act as if I had "something important to say." "Getting my intellectual act together" means that I finally freed myself from that predicament. In an incautious moment I promised Grazia that I would produce one more collage, an entire book, no less, on the topic of *reality*—and now I am stuck with it.

I don't mind. Writing has become a very pleasurable activity, almost like composing a work of art. There is some overall pattern, very vague at first, but sufficiently well defined to provide me with a starting point. Then come the details—arranging the words in sentences and paragraphs. I choose my words very carefully—they must sound right, must have the right rhythm, and their meaning must be slightly off center; nothing dulls the mind as thoroughly as a sequence of familiar notions. Then comes the story. It should be interesting and comprehensible, and it should have some unusual twists. I avoid "systematic" analyses. The elements hang together beautifully, but the argument itself is from outer space, as it were, unless it is connected with the lives and interests of individuals or special groups. Of course, it is already so connected, otherwise it would not be understood, but the connection is concealed, which means that, strictly speaking, a "systematic" analysis is a fraud. So why not avoid the fraud by using stories right away?

The problem of reality, on the other hand, always had a special fascination for me. Why are so many people dissatisfied with what they can see and feel? Why do they look for surprises behind events? Why do they believe that, taken together, these surprises form an entire world, and why, most strangely, do they take it for granted that this hidden world is more solid, more trustworthy, more "real" than the world from which they started? The search for surprises is natural; after all, what looked like one thing often turns out to be another. But why assume that all phenomena deceive and that (as Democritus claimed) "truth lies hidden in the abyss"?

In a way realists are like archaeologists, who, having removed layers of familiar and already boring events, find unexpected and unusual treasures. The treasures unearthed by science seem to have an additional advantage: being related to each other in lawful ways they can be manipulated or predicted by using the laws. But that makes them important only if the resulting scenario is pleasant to live in. The objection that the scenario is "real," and that we must adapt to it no matter what, has no weight, for it is not the only one: there are many ways of thinking and living.

A pluralism of this kind was once called irrational and was expelled from decent society. In the meantime it has become the fashion. This vogue did not make pluralism better or more humane; it made it trivial and, in the hands of its more learned defenders, scholastic. People, intellectuals especially, seem unable to be content with a little more freedom, a little more happiness, a little more light. Perceiving a small advantage, they seize it, circumscribe it, nail it down, and in this way prepare a New Age of ignorance, darkness, and slavery. It is rather surprising that there are still people who want to help others for personal reasons, because they are kind-hearted and not because they have been intimidated by principles. It is even more surprising that some of these people can work in institutions despite the greed, the incompetence, the power struggles that seem to surround the noblest cause. But there are such people, and my wife, Grazia, is one of them.

14   Marriage and Retirement

Grazia had been working in Rome; she has a large apartment near the university with a roof garden and exquisite furniture. I spent the final years of my academic career teaching in Zurich, and I am still ensconced in a small attic in Meilen, on Lake Zurich. We are not living together permanently—not yet. However, I often visit Grazia and she occasionally visits me. I have just returned from Rome. We had breakfast and lunch in the warm October air, surrounded by flowers, inspected by wasps who had built a nest right above our heads, and watched by a stern madonna in an alcove before us. In November (1993) we shall have been together for ten years; we have been married for five. Yet when arriving in Rome I felt as if I were visiting a woman I had just met and had fallen in love with. How will she look? I asked myself. How will she receive me? What will be the mood of the days ahead? It seems incredible that there was a time when I felt confined and tried to escape. The problem was in my imagination entirely—Grazia is a very independent person. She was saddened by my actions, but she faced them with a mixture of humor, tolerance, and determination. Without that, our lives would have parted and I would never have learned what it means to truly love a person.

We met by sheer accident. In the spring of 1983, Grazia tells me, she was on a train, traveling through Germany. Two men burst into her compartment, carrying skis and other alpine equipment and bringing with them a load of fresh mountain air. They started talking. Grazia mentioned that she was on her way to Berkeley. "Then you've got to see Feyerabend," one of them is supposed to have said; "he must be a very exciting person."

I did not at all feel "exciting" when I began my seminar that fall. I was bored. As is my custom, I walked in, sat down, pulled out my pocket calendar, turned to the person next to me, and asked, "Well, how are you going to entertain us?" That always causes surprise and dismay. Some students look furtively at the door, others try to make themselves invisible. Eventually they calm down and seem to enjoy the proceedings. Having finished my notes, I said goodbye and left. Grazia had not come to the first seminar.

She was late for the second one. That, I soon realized, was going to be the rule. Toward the end of the semester she told me how disappointed she had been. She had expected breathtaking performances by this allegedly "exciting" person, but all she got was student papers interrupted here and there by student questions while I hardly said a word. It was her own fault. I did talk, occasionally, during the first five to ten minutes. When I had become aware of Grazia, I often wished she were there. "She would be impressed," I thought while explaining some fascinating ideas of my own. Still, she came every time—if late.

After a few weeks we started talking to each other. I was rather pleased when I ran into her at the southeastern corner of the library. It happened so suddenly that I just said hello and moved on. I wished I had stopped for a little chat. I did stop and we did chat at the supermarket on Cedar and Shattuck, where I used to buy food. "Where do you live?" I asked. "It's a small street—you won't know it," she replied. "Tell me." "Miller Avenue"—it was just around the corner from my own place. Yet we had never met because we took different roads to town. Now we went to lunch and dinner, to movies and the theater, and for extended walks in the Berkeley hills.

Grazia wanted to have children. She said so during the first few days of our relationship. I said no. Not only that—the whole thing sounded like a message from another world. Me? A family? Children? Not on this planet!

Gradually my attitude changed. Reason had nothing to do with it. On the contrary, reason produced and kept producing excellent arguments against becoming a father. But I seemed to understand in a direct and intuitive way what children meant to Grazia, and I started feeling almost as she did. Emotional resonance, not intellectual insight, brought me around. We were married in January 1989, in Berkeley, as soon as we both felt ready to have children.

Being impotent I needed the aid of a physician. I traveled to Rome once a month, now hoping for success, now afraid of it. We tried, I believe, eight times. Then my prostate gland rebelled. I had had infections before, but I had been able to treat them with a variety of antibiotics. This time the standard drugs did not work. I had fever, pains, the shakes. I continued with my usual business of writing, buying food, cooking, washing my clothes. Seized by the shakes while driving, I ran into a wall and wrecked the car. My doctor sent me straight to the hospital. It took three weeks to tame the infection and a further week to eliminate the prostate. With that, our already very small chances of having a child went down to practically zero. But we have not given up.

In the fall of 1989 an earthquake hit the Bay area. I had just finished lecturing and was walking toward my car. There was a single jolt—nothing else. Inside the administration building a large chandelier started oscillating. People stopped, looked around, didn't know what to make of it. On the way home I saw fire engines moving downtown. "This small earthquake can't have started a fire," I said to myself. My house was unchanged except that a few small objects had fallen off the table. A huge cloud hovered over Berkeley. I turned to the television; ABC had no lights, but a few ghostly figures spoke of major damage. Gradually the picture emerged: a highway collapsed, fire on the San Francisco waterfront, all of San Francisco without electricity, large disruptions farther south. Sitting on top of the Berkeley hills I had a panoramic view of the catastrophe. Then came predictions of another and an even bigger earthquake. I decided to leave. I was not afraid of the earthquake itself but of the chaos afterward: no water, no food, no electricity for weeks. I sold some of my books, packed others, arranged with Janet, the chair of our department, to make my final decision in March 1990—and left for Switzerland.

When the fateful day arrived, I was tired and out of sorts. As always it was not reason but my mood that decided the case. I also felt that having made such a fuss about departing, I could hardly return with my tail between my legs. I resigned. A year later I was pensioned off in Switzerland as well (at Berkeley I could have continued indefinitely). And so, at long last, my childish wish became reality: I was a retired person.

I forgot the thirty-five years of my academic career almost as quickly as I had forgotten my military service. I find it hard to believe that only five years ago I was teaching at two academic institutions, one in Europe, the other in California; that a little earlier I had had tenure at four universities, Yale among them; and that it had been up to me and not to committees to accept or reject further offers. I am still as undefined, professionally and in character, as I was when entering the business, and I am amazed when interviewers treat me as if I were an oracle, a shaper of ideas, a friend or a foe of important movements, tendencies, institutions. Even my writings surprise me. Did I really write that? I ask myself. And in almost faultless American English?

There are times when I have a feeling of immense freedom. Now at last I can follow my inclinations without being hindered by a schedule and administrative rules. At other times I regret my decision. One reason is financial: it is always better to have a job than to be on a pension. Besides, my inclinations were never well defined. I am "free," yes, but does that give me a direction? It was easier when I had to set a few hours a week aside for my so-called job. Still, I'm convinced I did the right thing.

I'm a little more intelligent than I used to be; I've learned a few tricks, I'm better balanced, emotionally (though this balance still leaves much to be desired); in short, I'm in a much better position to start my life than I was only a decade ago—but I'm at the end of it, give or take a few years. Five years, perhaps, ten years if I'm lucky. That gives me pause. And why? Not because I would like to live forever, and certainly not because of the important books and papers that might remain unwritten, but because I would have liked to grow old with Grazia, because I would have liked to love her old and wrinkled face as I am loving her youthful face today, because I would have liked to support her in her troubles and to rejoice with her in her happy times. These thoughts, which start clamoring for attention whenever I think about the rest of my life, make it clear to me that there are strong inclinations after all, that they are not about abstract things such as solitude or intellectual achievements but about a live human being, and that at long last I have learned what it means to love somebody. I have certainly changed. I would not have changed had I continued with my Berkeley job. I would have been too distracted, I would have had too many escape routes, and I would have lacked the long days with Grazia that turned me from an icy egotist into a friend, a companion, a husband.

Most people put a distance between themselves and their surroundings. Western civilization as a whole turns humans into "individuals." I am I and you are you; we may love each other, but still I shall remain I and you will remain you. Like bulletproof glass, the fact that the parties to an exchange have an existence of their own puts limits on their feelings and actions.

In my case the limits were rather precisely drawn. Even as a child I had pushed my parents away. Later, when living with my father, I paid little attention to his fears and difficulties. I was annoyed when he fell sick, and I left him to the unfriendly care of his ladyfriends. I didn't visit him when he was dying. I felt uneasy from time to time, and I often desired a closer connection with parents, acquaintances, even with strangers. During my first days in the army I realized how cold I had been, and I decided to be a better son when I returned. I had good intentions but knew that they wouldn't last. One reason why I enjoyed the company of intelligent women was that they, their thoughts, their ways of approaching the world were less well defined than mine, because talking to them seemed to dissolve the boundaries between thought and emotion, knowledge and fiction, serious and more lighthearted matters, and because I myself became less well defined as a result. I was also influenced by Robin, who started out as my teaching assistant and then became a lifelong friend. He convinced me that there was no need to be afraid of strangers; he acted as if he had known them for years. Imitating him, I found that even a grim face might break out in a radiant smile over a joke or a friendly gesture. And I learned a lot from Spund.

Barbara had selected Spund from a litter of five. "I shall do all the work," she said when I pointed out that a puppy needs loads of attention. Things did not turn out that way. It was I who prepared his special calcium-enriched meals; it was I who removed the products of his (in)digestion, opened the door when he got restless during the day, during the night, anytime. Barbara called the dog Rommel. She didn't know very much about Rommel, the German war hero. She hadn't even seen a picture of him. But she seemed to like the sound of the name and the Hollywood myth that surrounded it. Somehow the name seemed to fit an image she had of herself—unapproachably beautiful, in her sports car, the unapproachably noble dog behind her. Things didn't turn out

that way either. Rommel was a German shepherd. But his ears
never stood up; he continued to urinate in a squatting position as
puppies do, rather than raising his hind leg haughtily like other
male dogs; and he ran after every person in sight. In a way, he had
no character, at least from Barbara's point of view. Moreover, he
threw up prodigiously during our trip to Denver. I rechristened
him Spund, a contraction of the dialect word *speiben,* which
means to vomit, and *Hund,* which means dog. (Spund is also the
name of a character in one of Nestroy's plays.)

Spund and I became close friends. I took him on excursions,
played with him, and often talked to him about the vagaries of
life. Spund understood what I said—he picked up the emotional
undercurrent in no time. He sensed the smallest change of my
mood and immediately displayed any mood of his own; there was
no control, no screening, no keeping up of pretenses. It was as if
Nature herself were talking directly to me. Occasionally I put on
old clothes and we fought, quite fiercely. A gesture—and we were
friends again. All this was the result of sympathy, not of training.
Nothing was hidden, everything was manifest. I was amazed, and
again some of the more solid layers of my character dissolved.

In 1974, while in London, I saw an excellent performance of
Richard II with Ian Richardson in the title role and Pasco as Boling-
brook. The director had read Ernst Kantorowicz's study *The King's
Two Bodies* and had arranged the action accordingly. I didn't know
that; nor did I know the book; and I saw the scene in which Richard (in Kantorowicz's words) "releases his body politic into thin
air" in a very different way.

> Now mark me how I will undo myself:
> I give this heavy weight from off my head,
> And this unwieldy scepter from my hand,
> The pride of kingly sway from out my heart;
> With mine own tears I wash away my balm,

With mine own hands I give away my crown,
With mine own tongue deny my sacred state,
With mine own breath release all dureous oaths:
All pomp and majesty do I forswear.

When Ian Richardson, speaking these lines, slowly dropped his shining golden cloak, his insignia, and all the things that had made him king, he seemed to be abandoning not just a social role but his very individuality, those features of his character that separated him from others; and the dark, unwieldy, clumsy, helpless creature that appeared seemed freer and safer, despite prison and death, than what he had left behind. I felt relieved, almost happy, as if my life had been renewed. It was not; I soon fell back into my old habits. But another experience had been added to my mental furniture.

I started talking about this experience, but abstractly and with some violence. I explained, in my lectures and on paper, that searching for the truth within the confines of a particular profession such as physics or philosophy, or doing our duty to family, fatherland, and humanity, does not exhaust our being, and that the sum of our works and/or deeds does not constitute a life. These activities and results, I said, are like debris on an ocean. They may coagulate and give better support to those who regard them as essential. They may even form a solid platform, thus creating an illusion of universality, security, and permanence. Yet the security and the permanence can be swept away in no time by the powers that permitted them to arise. I felt that writing papers and giving lectures was one thing, and living was another, and I advised students to seek their center of gravity outside whatever profession they might choose. It was in this connection that I ridiculed the notion of intellectual property and the standards that force a writer to refer the most insignificant intellectual fart to its proper source. I knew that refusing to define my life in terms of a profession or specific actions did not yet give it content, but at least I was aware that there was such a content apart from this or that particular activity. I was aware, but I was not particularly concerned. At any rate, I felt no urge to pursue the matter.

Today it seems to me that love and friendship play a central role and that without them even the noblest achievements and the most fundamental principles remain pale, empty, and dangerous. And when speaking of love, I don't mean an abstract commitment such as a "love of truth" or a "love of humanity," which, taken by themselves, have often encouraged narrow-mindedness and cruelty. Nor do I mean emotional fireworks that soon exhausted themselves. I can't really say what I mean, for that would delimit a phenomenon that is a constantly changing mixture of concern and illumination. Love lures people out of their limited "individuality," it expands horizons, and it changes every object in their way. Yet there is no merit in this kind of love. It is subjected neither to the intellect nor to the will; it is the result of a fortunate constellation of circumstances. It is a gift, not an achievement.

In 1991 I saw a movie, *Martha und Ich,* by Jiri Weiss, with Marianne Sägebrecht and Michel Piccoli. It's the story of a boy who, having been seduced by the family maid, is shipped off to his uncle, a famous gynecologist. But the uncle, instead of preaching reform, introduces the boy to erotic drawings and mature books. He has a beautiful wife, much younger than he. He chases her away when he returns from a conference to find her in bed with a man of her own age. Both wife and lover leave the house half naked —to the boy's amazement and, we may assume, further education. The gynecologist marries his housekeeper, Martha, a kind but ungainly woman. His relatives revolt: a common woman, a mere housekeeper, becoming part of an uncommon family? After the wedding, the gynecologist meets Martha's family—two brothers, both peasants. One of the brothers becomes offensive; the gynecologist is a Jew, the brother an anti-Semite. I still remember the strange feeling I had at this point. I had identified with the man, I was completely on his side. Now he seemed a marked person. For them? For me? If for me, did this mean that the anti-Semitic rhetoric that had surrounded me for years had not been without effect?

The gynecologist loses patients. A Star of David is painted on the wall of his house. This simple event, which was over in a few minutes, made a deep impression on me. For the first time I *felt*, to a small degree, what it meant to be branded as an outcast. I had not understood such events before, I had not even noticed them. True, I had burst into tears at age nine over *Uncle Tom's Cabin*, and I had shuddered when reading how innocence, hope, goodness, how entire lives, were destroyed by hatred, greed, and selfishness. But these had been scattered reactions, unconnected with thought or a coherent emotional or moral character. Now a long life and the good fortune of having met Grazia had given me at least a trace of such a character, something to start from, something to give shape to the rest of my existence.

Looking back at this episode, I conclude that a moral character cannot be created by argument, "education," or an act of will. It cannot be created by any kind of planned action, whether scientific, political, moral, or religious. Like true love, it is a gift, not an achievement. It depends on accidents such as parental affection, some kind of stability, friendship, and—following therefrom—on a delicate balance between self-confidence and a concern for others. We can create conditions that favor the balance; we cannot create the balance itself. Guilt, responsibility, obligation—these ideas make sense when the balance is given. They are empty words, even obstacles, when it is lacking.

But what can we do in an age like ours that has not yet achieved that balance? What can we do while our criminals, their judges and henchmen, while the philosophers, poets, prophets who try to force us into their patterns, and while we, who are collaborators or victims or simply bystanders, are still in a barbaric state? The answer is obvious: with a few exceptions we shall act in a barbaric way. We shall punish, kill, meet violence with violence, pit teachers against students, set "intellectual leaders" against the public and against each other; we shall speak about transgressions in resounding moral terms and demand that violations of the law be prevented by force. But while continuing our own lives in this manner, we should at least try to give our children a chance. We should offer them love and security, not principles, and under no circumstances should we burden them with the crimes of the past. They may have to deal for generations with the physical, juridical, and financial consequences of our actions and with the chaos we leave behind; but they are free of any moral, historical, national guilt. As for myself—I certainly cannot undo my wavering and unconcern during the Nazi period. Nor do I think that I can be blamed or held responsible for my behavior. Responsibility assumes that we know the alternatives, that we know how to choose from among them, and that we use this knowledge to push them aside through cowardice, opportunism, or ideological fervor. But I can report what I thought and did, what I think about these thoughts and actions today, and why I changed.

Grazia read some of my articles and criticized them quite thoroughly—the language, the presentation, the ideas. Not a single page escaped her "non capisco." Much of my book *Farewell to Reason* (another collage) would be dreary and incomprehensible were it not for her gentle but determined interventions. I in turn read some of her work and made suggestions here and there. After ten years of such exchanges our views have become rather similar except that Grazia knows a wealth of details and has the ability, which I lack, to grasp the simple ideas behind a complex and murky message. She studied physics as I did, but went further —her degree is undiluted by philosophical admixtures. She had great talent in this subject, she was at the cutting edge of research, and a splendid career lay in front of her—some of her colleagues

even predicted a Nobel Prize. Yet she gave it all up. Having seen
human misery close up in India she wanted to do something to
relieve it, and physics, she thought, was not the right subject for
that. Guided more by intuition than by a clear plan, she moved to
Berkeley, found ways of getting a degree in public health, and
started a new career in conservation and development. Here she
adopted and continues to improve an approach called "primary
environmental care" (PEC), which treats environmental problems "from below," i.e. neither by global strategies nor on the
basis of programs worked out in distant offices, but in a case-by-
case manner, always remaining in close touch with the problems,
wishes, opinions of the local populations. She has visited communities in Ethiopia, Ecuador, Costa Rica, Brazil, Los Angeles(!),
Uganda, Tanzania, and other places. She recently became head of
the social policy program at the World Conservation Union
(IUCN) in Gland near Geneva. I admire her tremendously—her
intelligence, her perseverance, her strength in adversity—her
gentleness (which, incidentally, does not prevent her from being
quite pushy on occasions), and especially the way in which she
hides all these talents and achievements. For in personal contact
Grazia is as direct and as immediate as Spund used to be, and I
have often compared her to that gentle and trusting creature.
Is it surprising that I behave like a newlywed adolescent and
keep bothering friends, acquaintances, even total strangers, with
Grazia stories?

15   Fading Away

When I wrote down the title of this final chapter in the summer of 1993, I had in mind my *professional* fading away. No more papers, one short book to finish, occasional lectures to pay for some trips with Grazia. I expected to spend time reading, walking in the woods, and devoting myself to my wife. It didn't quite turn out that way.

In the early 1990s, Grazia and I attended a variety of conferences. In Florence I met old friends like Marcello Pera, Hilary Putnam, Bob Cohen, and Ian Hacking, and made new ones like Bas van Fraassen. One cold, windy evening we walked past the Duomo, which was magnificent. I had often talked with Grazia about the times in which Siena, Florence, Orvieto—relatively poor by modern standards, beset by wars, hit by incomprehensible diseases—managed to create such grandiose monuments. The spirit of those people, strengthened by their faith, is still in front of us, a living heart in the middle of a city. For the meeting in Florence I had prepared a written speech for publication—but I delivered it without a manuscript. The room was full of people who seemed to believe I was a star, something I just could not comprehend.

I also went to Locarno a few times, and once I gave a talk on the historical dimensions of rationalism. It was not a good talk—I read part of it, skipped lines here and there, and garbled it all in the process. In 1990 I was given the Premio Fregene, along with Alberto Moravia, the Prince of Wales, the author of a cookbook, and the author of a book on abuse of young girls. The prize, assigned each year for achievements in various fields, was for my latest collection of essays, *Farewell to Reason,* which had just appeared in Italian. My round-trip to Rome from Zurich was paid for, I received a small but heavy metal trophy, and I was interviewed for Italian television. At about the same time, Cardinal Ratzinger, the pope's expert on doctrinal affairs, gave a talk in Parma about Galileo and mentioned me in support of his views.

In Palermo for another meeting, we had dinner with Alain Robbe-Grillet, who was more interested in Grazia than in his fellow intellectuals. We were also invited to Spoleto, where they had added a philosophical appendix to Menotti's music festival. There, in 1991, Stephen Jay Gould told me he had drawn his ideas on punctuated equilibrium from *Against Method.* He gave a rousing speech along the lines of his book *Wonderful Life.* In 1993 we were in Spoleto a second time and listened to a magnificent performance of Berlioz's *Requiem* in front of the Duomo. At long last we also managed to attend a stage performance of *Gianni Schicchi,* one of our favorite operas. We had pleasant conversations with Jerome Bruner and heard a talk on chaos theory by John Barrow. As usual, I tried to deconstruct whatever grand concepts occurred in the talks and the debates. There were other trips—to the Netherlands, to Naples, to Vienna—and many peaceful days in Rome.

Sometime during these years I was invited to become a member of the editorial board of a new journal, *Common Knowledge,* published by Oxford University Press. In that function I had to write columns and "little reviews" for recently published books, which I ordered and received at no cost. I found the combination of rhetoric and argument inherent in writing columns very congenial—no long-drawn-out argumentation, but quick observations, held together by bits and pieces of reasoning. Images and cheeky remarks surrounded by thought, or thought spiced by cheek and images: a column is essentially a minestrone! Contrary to my past habits (for years I refused to be interviewed by the most respectable as well as the most disreputable journals and TV stations), I started giving interviews for various European journals and broadcast media, and even enjoyed it. I also began my autobiography, mainly to recall my time in the German army and the way I had experienced national socialism. This also proved a good way of explaining how my "ideas" were intertwined with the rest of my life.

I had promised Grazia a book on reality, which was very slowly taking shape. The working title is *Conquest of Abundance*. The book is intended to show how specialists and common people reduce the abundance that surrounds and confuses them, and the consequences of their actions. It is mainly a study of the role of abstractions—mathematical and physical notions especially— and of the stability and "objectivity" they seem to carry with them. It deals with the ways in which such abstractions arise, are supported by common ways of speaking and living, and change as a result of argumentation and/or practical pressure. In the book I also try to emphasize the essential ambiguity of all concepts, images, and notions that presuppose change. Without ambiguity, no change, ever. The quantum theory, as interpreted by Niels Bohr, is a perfect example of that.

Conquest of Abundance should be a simple book, pleasant to read and easy to understand. One of my motives for writing *Against Method* was to free people from the tyranny of philosophical obfuscators and abstract concepts such as "truth," "reality," or "objectivity," which narrow people's vision and ways of being in the world. Formulating what I thought were my own attitude and convictions, I unfortunately ended up by introducing concepts of similar rigidity, such as "democracy," "tradition," or "relative truth." Now that I am aware of it, I wonder how it happened. The urge to explain one's own ideas, not simply, not in a story, but by means of a "systematic account," is powerful indeed. How else can one explain how an outstanding theatrical director such as Herbert Blau—an artist capable of making opaque roles and plays clear to actors and audiences—can have produced a treatise on the theater that contains incomprehensible statements and plain nonsense? It is not a difficulty inherent in the subject matter. Plato, Aristotle, Brecht, and Dürrenmatt wrote about the theater in pleasing and comprehensible ways. It is the wish to be great, profound, and philosophical. But what is more important—to be understood by outsiders or to be regarded as a "deep thinker"? Writing in a simple style that general readers can understand is not the same as being superficial. I urge all writers who want to inform their fellow citizens to stay away from philosophy, or at least to stop being intimidated and influenced by obfuscators such as Derrida and, instead, to read Schopenhauer or Kant's popular essays.

By the end of 1993, the title of this chapter has assumed a new meaning. I am partially paralyzed, in a hospital, with an inoperable brain tumor.

I would not want to die now that I have finally got my act together—in my private as well as my professional life. I would like to stay with Grazia to support her and cheer her up when the business gets hairy (her business). After a life of fighting for solitude, I would like to live as part of a family, making my contribution along the way—like having dinner and a few jokes ready when she comes back from work. We might even try to use the most advanced methods of having children, but in the meantime we have to wait for the further development of my illness—not a pleasant position to be in, especially for Grazia, who had high hopes for a new life for us together. Writing columns for a journal may even have improved my writing style; the book I promised to her might even have turned out simple and rather luminous—it might have shown how reason and emotion can work together in a "scholarly" production.

Grazia is with me in the hospital, which is a great joy, and she fills the room with light. In one way I am ready to depart, despite all the things I still would like to do, but in another way I am sad to leave this beautiful world behind, especially Grazia, whom I would have liked to accompany for a few more years.

* * *

These may be the last days. We are taking them one at a time. My latest paralysis was the result of some bleeding inside the brain. My concern is that after my departure something remains of me, *not* papers, *not* final philosophical declarations, but love. I hope that that will remain and will not be too much affected by the manner of my final departure, which I would like to be peaceful, like a coma, without a death struggle, leaving bad memories behind. Whatever happens now, our small family can live forever —Grazia, me, and our love. That is what I would like to happen, not intellectual survival but the survival of love.

POSTSCRIPT

A couple of weeks after Paul wrote these words, the tumor began to affect the pain center in his brain, and he needed extremely high doses of morphine. He was accustomed to painkillers, having suffered excruciating pain all his life as a consequence of his war injury (pain, and the prodigious amount and variety of his reading, are important aspects of Paul's life hardly mentioned in the autobiography), but the doctors were still astounded that he was able to tolerate so much morphine and for so many days. On February 11, 1994, Paul had been in a sort of induced coma for more than a week. The mail brought a letter from the Italian publisher Laterza, saying that they were enthusiastic about the autobiography and ready to publish it very soon. I was anguished and exhausted, but I felt happy about the good news, and told Paul with joy in my voice. He was breathing slowly, and somehow peacefully. A few seconds later, he simply was not anymore. We were alone, holding hands, and it was midday.

Grazia Borrini Feyerabend